DOING BUSINESS IN
EASTERN EUROPE

Poland · Hungary · Czechoslovakia

Karen Liebreich

BBC BOOKS

To and with Jeremy, and many thanks to
Michael, Freddy and Kitty Liebreich.

Published by BBC Books,
a division of BBC Enterprises Limited,
Woodlands, 80 Wood Lane, London W12 0TT
First published 1991
© Karen Liebreich 1991
ISBN 0 563 36180 8
Designed by Graham Dudley Associates
Set in Baskerville by Butler and Tanner Ltd, Frome
Printed and bound in Great Britain by Butler and Tanner Ltd, Frome
Jacket printed by Belmont Press Ltd, Northampton

CONTENTS

AUTHOR'S NOTE

The term 'businessman' is used throughout the book, and needless to say implies no discrimination, but only reflects the irritating fact that the vast majority of the business people interviewed for this book were men. 'Western' is used in the broadest sense to mean non-communist, in other words capitalist, and includes Western Europe, the United States and Japan.

Currency conversions are a tricky issue. The many devaluations necessary since market forces began to affect the forint, zloty and crown mean that the rates are continually changing. Wherever possible, the rate relevant at the time has been given. If the sum refers to a fixed deposit necessary, for instance, to register a new company, this is often cited – even within the country itself – in dollars. The investor should of course check, since, in fast-changing circumstances, prices may have changed since the time of writing.

Every care has been taken to be accurate but statistics provided by communist governments were often unreliable.

SiE A

0 miles   100   200

0 km   160   320

International boundary —·—··—·—

POLAND

WARSAW

USSR

E

ECHOSLOVAKIA

CARPATHIAN MOUNTAINS

Bratislava

VIENNA

RIA

BUDAPEST

HUNGARY

ROMANIA

LOVENIA

CROATIA

BUCHAREST

BELGRADE

YUGOSLAVIA

BOSNIA AND
HERCEGOVINA

BULGARIA

SERBIA

DRIATIC SEA

MONTENEGRO

SOFIA

ALBANIA

MACEDONIA

GREECE

OPEN FOR BUSINESS

The Berlin Wall is nothing more than a crumbling souvenir on the mantlepiece of history. Europe is once more whole and 130 million people in Eastern Europe have rejoined the common European home. As communist central planners bury their five-year plans, a new vista opens up. A huge task of reconstruction, almost equal to that facing Europe after the Second World War, now faces the governments of Eastern Europe as they struggle with their outdated industries and poor infrastructure, hoping to pacify populations starved of democracy and consumer goods. After more than forty years of separation from Western Europe (ideological, political, economic, technological and physical) the borders have opened, and the years of neglect must be made good.

As the initial euphoria of liberty began to wane, the countries of Eastern Europe started to recognise the enormity of their task. It is one thing to throw out the five-year plans and proclaim the arrival of the free market, but much harder to acknowledge that what this means in reality is that your factory has for twenty years been producing useless and outdated goods of shoddy quality, and you are now one step from unemployment. Moreover you are suddenly paying real prices for foodstuffs, for the local bus, for petrol, for the rental of your flat, and as if this were not enough, inflation may well be adding to your woes. Initially the population of Eastern Europe seemed to comprehend this, acknowledging that it had to knuckle down and suffer for a while. Poland in 1990 was perhaps the prime example of this gritted acceptance, but no one knew how tough conditions might become, or how successful the results would be.

The changes in progress provide huge opportunities for Western businessmen. In 1990 phrases like 'the Eastern Klondyke' began to circulate, and big multinationals, smaller companies and those just out for a quick buck, began to investigate the market. According to an Institute of Directors survey carried out in spring 1990, 70% of British company directors expected to be doing business with Eastern Europe by 1992. Eighty-nine per cent of companies interviewed for another survey said that events in Eastern Europe would provide them with new business opportunities[1]. It is unde-niable that there are great opportunities for increased trade as a huge market of 130 million potential consumers press their noses to the window of a post-1992 European Community. Although the EC's population is only about twice the size of that of Eastern Europe it produces over ten times the output. And, not only in terms of consumers, but also as a source of manpower, Eastern Europe is attractive, with its literate, and at present cheap pool of labour.

In cultural terms the countries of Eastern, and especially Central, Europe are close to the countries of the European Community. Whether, like Romania, they formed part of the Roman Empire, or whether they were linked under the Holy Roman Empire of the Middle Ages, the Reformation and Counter-Reformation of the fifteenth, sixteenth and seventeenth centuries, or more recently under the Austro-Hungarian Empire, East and West Europe have a common heritage. Geographically the coun-tries are inextricably linked: towns have changed countries (for instance, Wrocław/Breslau) as national borders have shifted through the centuries. It has become a cliché to point out that Prague lies further to the West than Vienna, that Berlin is now closer to the centre of Europe than Brussels. 'Eastern Europe' lies almost in the heart of the continent, and businesses cannot afford to ignore the shift in emphasis as communication and distribution systems re-adjust to these new realities in the last decade of the twentieth century.

Three countries, Hungary, Poland and Czechoslovakia, together represent the area which is of the greatest interest to Western businessmen. The rest of Eastern and Central Europe lags some way behind these three countries, in terms of political development, of commitment to economic reform of the most wide-ranging sort, and of the level of interest which its industries and market can arouse amongst Western businessmen.

Bulgaria, for instance, took steps towards creating a market economy after the fall of Todor Zhivkov in November 1989 after thirty-five years in power. Foreign trade was actively encouraged, enterprises were expected to try to make a profit and Bulgaria sought membership of the International Monetary Fund. Tra-ditionally the country specialised in construction of transportation and agricultural equipment, with some electronics. According to Zhivkov's replacement, Petar Mladenov, however, the economy in November 1989 was on the verge of cardiac arrest. Industrial machinery was outdated, inflation was rising, the foreign debt was over $10 billion, there were ecological problems and agricultural production had fallen in recent years. The population of nearly 9 million includes 10% Turks, and in 1989 there were significant nationalist clashes between Turks and ethnic Bulgarians. Elections in June 1990 resulted in a political stalemate with the opposition Union of Democratic Forces reluctant to co-operate with the Communist party, now renamed the Socialist party, which had achieved the doubtful honour of being the only Communist party in Eastern Europe to be re-elected. In November 1990, economic protests forced the Socialists to resign, leaving an independent caretaker government. Political uncertainties, economic poverty and the relatively small size of the market mean that Bulgaria has so far failed to attract much Western business interest.

Just north of Bulgaria lies Romania, where an even less attractive business environment prevails. Western observers, politicians and businessmen alike, have yet to decide their policies towards the government, the National Salvation Front. The country has a population of 23 million, including 2 million predominantly disaffected Hungarians. Over the last decades industry was mainly geared towards engineering and metallurgy, with a nod towards light industry such as textile production. Statistics on economic performance through the 1970s and 1980s, however, are so unreliable as to be worthless, except perhaps as exhibits in a museum of propaganda. Nicolae Ceauşescu, once the West's most favoured 'good Communist', was executed in Eastern Europe's most bloody coup in December 1989. He had come to power in 1965 and won the approval and support of the West by pursuing an independent line: he did not condemn Israel in 1967, and he refused to participate in, or condone, the suppression of the Prague Spring by Warsaw Pact forces in 1968. In 1972 Romania joined the International Monetary Fund, in 1973 it was awarded preferential trading status with the Common Market, two years later the United States gave it 'most-favoured nation status', and in 1978 the Queen awarded Ceauşescu the Order of the Bath.

By the 1980s though, the gloss had begun to fade. Ceauşescu was determined to repay the rescheduled foreign debt of over $10 billion and in early 1989 announced that this had been achieved. It was, however, at the cost of rationing everything from meat to petrol and electricity, and by restricting investment in the industrial base. Dissent was brutally suppressed, but finally erupted in Timişoara, where the ethnic Hungarian majority of Transylvania had long been unhappy over the suppression of their culture, and more recently over the policy of 'systematisation', whereby villages were to be forcibly moved and combined into larger urban centres.

After Ceauşescu's summary execution the National Salvation Front was established, but within a month the most respected ex-dissidents, such as Doina Cornea, had resigned, leaving Ion Iliescu, a former colleague of Ceauşescu's, in control. Elections held in May 1990 confirmed him as president with Petre Roman as prime minister. How fair the elections were remains a matter of discussion, but Iliescu's behaviour before and since caused the West to delay aid and encouragement. To exiled Romanians the government represents nothing but 'recycled *nomenklatura*' and is regarded with deep mistrust. The problem of the Hungarian minority in Romania has not been resolved and continues to provide a source of friction. Although the government has declared itself keen to promote Western involvement and has introduced some legislation, for instance making it easier for Western companies to invest in local enterprises, Romania remains very much on probation. New legislation was drawn up in October 1990 aimed at attracting foreign investment by offering tax holidays and permitting repatriation of profits, but in a country of such poverty and with such pressing economic problems, the accusations of human rights abuses and the threat of political instability have effectively extinguished Western business interest.

Such interest has never been lacking in Yugoslavia, although recently the political situation has been far from clear, with the country apparently in the process of breaking up into its constituent republics. With the decline of communism, Yugoslavia, with its 23 million population, has been left at a political crossroads. The country was created in 1918 as a federation of six republics – roughly from north to south, Slovenia, Croatia, Bosnia Herzegovina, Serbia, Montenegro and Macedonia – and two autonomous regions – Kosovo and Vojvodina. The republics underwent considerable decentralisation in the mid 1970s, which resulted in some duplication, especially in industry. Predominant exports are industrial, and Yugoslavia is one of Europe's leading suppliers of copper, silver, mercury and bauxite. The main industries are concentrated in mining, food processing, metal-working, electrical machinery and equipment. After the death in 1980 of Marshal Tito the binding force that had kept such diverse republics together disappeared. Unemployment and hyper-inflation began to disrupt the economy and nationalism became a serious problem.

Slovenia, the most 'Central European' of the republics and economically the most advanced, increasingly saw itself as subsidising the rest of the country, and as the economy declined and the wave of nationalism grew, it became more and more reluctant to do so. Worries about rule by Serbia led this predominantly Catholic republic to amend its constitution to permit secession if necessary. In the elections in May 1990 it retained a communist president, but voted in a centre-right government.

Serbia, the largest republic, is an ex-kingdom with an Eastern Orthodox population. Nationalism flourished here as Serbia felt increasingly frustrated by having only one vote in Yugoslavia's affairs, although so much larger and potentially more powerful than the other republics in the federation. While about 5 million Serbs live in Serbia itself, another 3.5 million live elsewhere within the republic, providing a handy pretext for nationalist complaints. In Kosovo, once the heartland of Serbian culture, the Moslem Albanian population, with its far higher birthrate began to threaten the Serbian population, causing riots and tension throughout the late 1980s. In December 1990, Serbia elected the communist – renamed socialist – president, Slobodan Milosevic, on a fiercely nationalist platform. Fears of a greater Serbia sent shivers through Slovenia and Croatia.

Croatia, sandwiched between Slovenia and Serbia, and increasingly drawn towards Slovenia, elected a right-wing nationalist government in May 1990. In December it passed a new constitution declaring itself a sovereign republic. The smaller Yugoslav republics have also been afflicted by the same economic malaise, but being poorer and more dependent on subsidies from their larger partners, have remained more passive politically, and have divided their sympathies accordingly.

In 1985 legislation was introduced to facilitate an integrated Yugoslav market with, for instance, incentives for private enterprise. In practice, however, hyper-inflation (officially calculated at 1,225% in 1989), unemployment and duplication of resources in each republic badly affected the economy.

Through the 1980s, Yugoslavia was economically and politically more liberated than the rest of Eastern Europe, and was as a result relatively attractive to Western investors. Unfortunately, the political stalemate between the republics has been reflected in the economic environment. The Yugoslav federation has become so loose that it will be forced either to reform itself or break up into its constituent parts. The brave Western investor is either obliged to contend with negotiating with institutions which may have only a limited existence, or wait until the political climate resolves itself in one way or another. Potentially, however, sections of the Yugoslav economy, especially in the northern republics, are of interest to Western investors.

The same cannot be said of Albania, which has very little of interest for Western businessmen. A predominantly rural country, Albania is the most backward and primitive country in Europe, with the lowest standard of living, and a very poorly educated population. Agriculture accounts for 25% of all exports and the country is almost self-sufficient in food, with only about 35% of the 3 million population living in towns. The country exports oil, minerals (especially chromium), metals, textiles and electricity, mainly to other Eastern European countries, but the policy under Enver Hoxha, who was in power from 1945 until his death in 1985, was totally isolationist. Under his successors, Albania has begun to open the door to the rest of the world. Diplomatic links were established with Spain in 1986 and the following year with West Germany. In December 1989 a slight economic liberalisation meant that, for instance, some privatisation of livestock farming was permitted, and some prices were no longer centrally controlled. Demonstrations in early 1990 were followed by a flood of requests for emigration, and a subsequent political retrenchment. Economic reforms continued, and a decree was promulgated in July 1990 permitting foreign investment in the country. Joint ventures were also given a legal footing. However, the economic situation remains very regulated, and the size and quality of Albania's market is such that Western interest and investment is extremely limited. In December 1990, after demonstrations and riots, opposition political parties were finally permitted, with free elections to follow.

At the opposite end of the scale from Albania lay East Germany, once considered the most successful East European economy. Now absorbed into the Federal Republic, it has slid into the European Community and its economic problems have become part of the new Germany's. Investment there has naturally been dominated by German business, and the opportunities offered by East Germany lie outside the scope of this book. So too do those offered by the Soviet Union, which is a country covering such a vast area, of such diversity, that it would be too simplistic to discuss and dismiss in a few lines. The situation in the Soviet Union is very different from that in Eastern Europe, in that the Communist party (at least at the time of writing) is still in power, and is seeking a way to reform the country without relinquishing its grip. Although many business opportunities in the Soviet Union do exist, the approach needed to exploit them is very different from that required in Eastern Europe. Suffice it to say that if, as the saying goes, every change is an opportunity for someone, then there are many opportunities in the Soviet Union for the business-man who can take advantage of them.

Czechoslovakia, Hungary and Poland, the heartland of Eastern – or as these countries themselves prefer to be known, Central – Europe, taken as a whole represent perhaps the most interesting and accessible area for Western businessmen. All three countries had a somewhat similar economic structure. All three were members of the Council for Mutual Economic Assistance, CMEA or Comecon. This was created in 1949 to facilitate economic integration among the Soviet satellite countries. It included the European Eastern Bloc (Bulgaria, Czechoslovakia, East Germany, Hungary, Poland, Romania) and was later joined by Mongolia (1961), Cuba (1972) and Vietnam (1978). For the first twenty years or so of its existence it was relatively efficient, especially in the field of heavy industry. However, modernisation of technology and local standards of living suffered, and with the fall of the Berlin Wall, Comecon seemed destined either for complete extinction or for total reform. In January 1990 the Czechoslovak finance minister, Václav Klaus, announced that the organisation had lost its *raison d'être* and could no longer exist in its present form. Since all business is now to be conducted in bilateral agreements or in convertible currency, much of Comecon's relevance had evaporated.

Comecon was never a Common Market; it was rather an economic grouping whereby different states specialised in the production of various materials. Basically, the system revolved around the exchange of oil products and raw materials from the Soviet Union to its satellite states who responded with a supply of industrial, agricultural and consumer products. Pricing of products was worked out in a convoluted manner, loosely based on average world prices over the preceding five years and always expressed in the paper currency of Comecon, transferable roubles. Debts and compensation were organised through a central bank, but those countries such as Czechoslovakia who were owed large sums, lost out since they could not charge interest, convert the debt into goods or hard currency, or use it to repay a third country. Meanwhile the Soviet Union was selling its oil at an unrealistic price – either too high or too low, depending on the rest of the market. The USSR also lost out since the machinery it was obliged to 'buy' from its partners, at unrealistic prices, was of poor quality and low technology.

The disadvantages attached to this system encouraged Comecon countries to try and increase their external trade, and with the collapse of central planning, Comecon as it stood became totally unworkable. This was recognised at a meeting of the members held in the Bulgarian capital Sofia in January 1990. The Czechoslovaks, Hungarians and Poles wanted to abolish the system almost immediately, although they realised they would experience difficulties paying in hard currency. They were not to know that the Gulf Crisis would soon exacerbate these difficulties. Eventually the suggestion by the Soviet Union, which would have perhaps most to gain from the successful reform of Comecon, to conduct all transactions at world prices and in convertible currency from 1991, was accepted[2]. Even after Comecon countries began trading at world prices on 1 January 1991 some transactions were still settled using the old system because of lack of adequate hard currency. Comecon's administration was reduced; it was renamed the Organisation for International Economic Co-operation, and sought to redefine its role.

Meanwhile the Eastern European countries remained dependent on the Soviet Union for their energy supplies, and the Gulf conflict, which drastically affected the price per barrel, proved a devastating blow to Eastern Europe. Even without this development, the shift to hard-currency accounting for oil supplies was already expected to swallow up a huge proportion of precious hard-currency reserves.

The Soviet Union's supplies of oil had always been somewhat unreliable, but in mid 1990 the situation became more critical with the USSR reneging on delivery contracts to the three countries, and cutting around 30% of promised tonnage. A report issued by the EC in October 1990 estimated that the increased price of oil due to the Gulf conflict would cost Eastern Europe nearly $7 billion in 1990, and more in 1991. Eastern Europe may yet regret the demise of Comecon.

On the other side of the disintegrated Iron Curtain another organisation which faced an uncertain future was CoCom, the Co-ordinating Committee for Multilateral Export Controls, which restricted access of Western technology to the 'hostile' Eastern Bloc. Although the United States remained keen to retain some controls, by July 1990 the list of industrial products subject to controls had been cut by one third.

The loss of East Germany, one of Eastern Europe's main trading partners, also hit Czechoslovakia, Hungary and Poland hard. In August 1990 alone East Germany cancelled large-scale contracts with Czechoslovakia worth 230 million roubles (officially $450 million), and this was just a foretaste of the effect that Germany's unification was to have on its neighbours.

*   *   *

The historical, political and economic development of Czechoslovakia, Hungary and Poland are discussed in some depth in the first three chapters of this book. Chapter 4 goes into greater detail as to the advantages and disadvantages of each of these countries and looks at some areas of interest to Western investors. Chapter 5 discusses the legislation which has been enacted in each country to attract foreign investment. The situation is still changing rapidly and issues such as privatisation, ownership rights and joint venture possibilities are examined. Chapter 6 looks at the reaction in the West to the developments in Eastern Europe, whether in the form of initial aid, know-how funds or specific grants. There are many practical difficulties to working in these countries, particularly linked to the underdeveloped infrastructure, and some suggestions are offered in Chapter 7.

The book concludes with a directory of useful contacts, both in Britain and in the countries in question. The businessman is strongly advised to consult these for the latest information, since in such a fluid situation changes are occurring all the time.

When I first started researching for the BBC's *Business Matters* series on *Doing Business in Eastern Europe* in spring 1990, I was invited to attend a number of conferences and seminars. In almost every case the room prepared for the meeting proved too small and the amount of interest clearly surprised the organisers. Audiences for lectures on investment possibilities in Eastern Europe had suddenly increased tenfold. Flights to Warsaw had once been half empty, now the business section has swelled to bursting point. Hotels in Prague had once been easy to book, now a tent is beginning to seem the only option. Most of the investors flocking towards the new markets have never even been to Eastern Europe before, although many have had experience of working in European Community countries. This book is aimed at those who are approaching these markets, who have heard of Lech Walesa but are not sure about Jan Masaryk or Jozsef Antall, who can maybe cope with French but not Magyar. Unlike France or Germany, Eastern Europe has until now been off the beaten track for businessmen. Recent events, however, have changed this irrevocably – the map must now be redrawn.

CHAPTER 1

CZECHOSLOVAKIA

Official name	*The Czech and Slovak Federated Republic*
Area	*127,870 km²*
Population	*15,620,000 (1988)*
Capital	*Prague*
Currency	*koruna (crown)*

HISTORY, GEOGRAPHY AND POLITICS

Czechoslovakia is bordered by Germany, Poland, the Soviet Union, Hungary and Austria. It is made up of three provinces, Bohemia, Moravia and Slovakia, with a population of 15.6 million. Although land-locked, it has access to the North Sea via the Elbe, and the Danube which flows east to the Black Sea. The north-east of the country is mountainous with walking and skiing in the Tatra and Beskidy areas.

Prague is the national capital, culturally and administratively. Bratislava, less than half the size of Prague, is the capital of Slovakia and seat of the Slovak state government. Brno is Moravia's main city, while much of the province's industry is situated around Ostrava, where you can feel the coal dust settling in your hair and lungs.

The country acquired its present borders in 1948. Under the tenth-century ruler, Boleslav I, Bohemia was forced to join the Holy Roman Empire and Prague became an important trading centre. By the early twelfth century the Kingdom of Bohemia was an important power in the region. The death of the last local ruler in the early fourteenth century precipitated a time of unrest, but in 1310 the Bohemian Estates elected John of Luxembourg as their new king. His son, Charles IV, later Holy Roman Emperor, made Prague into the most important cultural centre in the region.

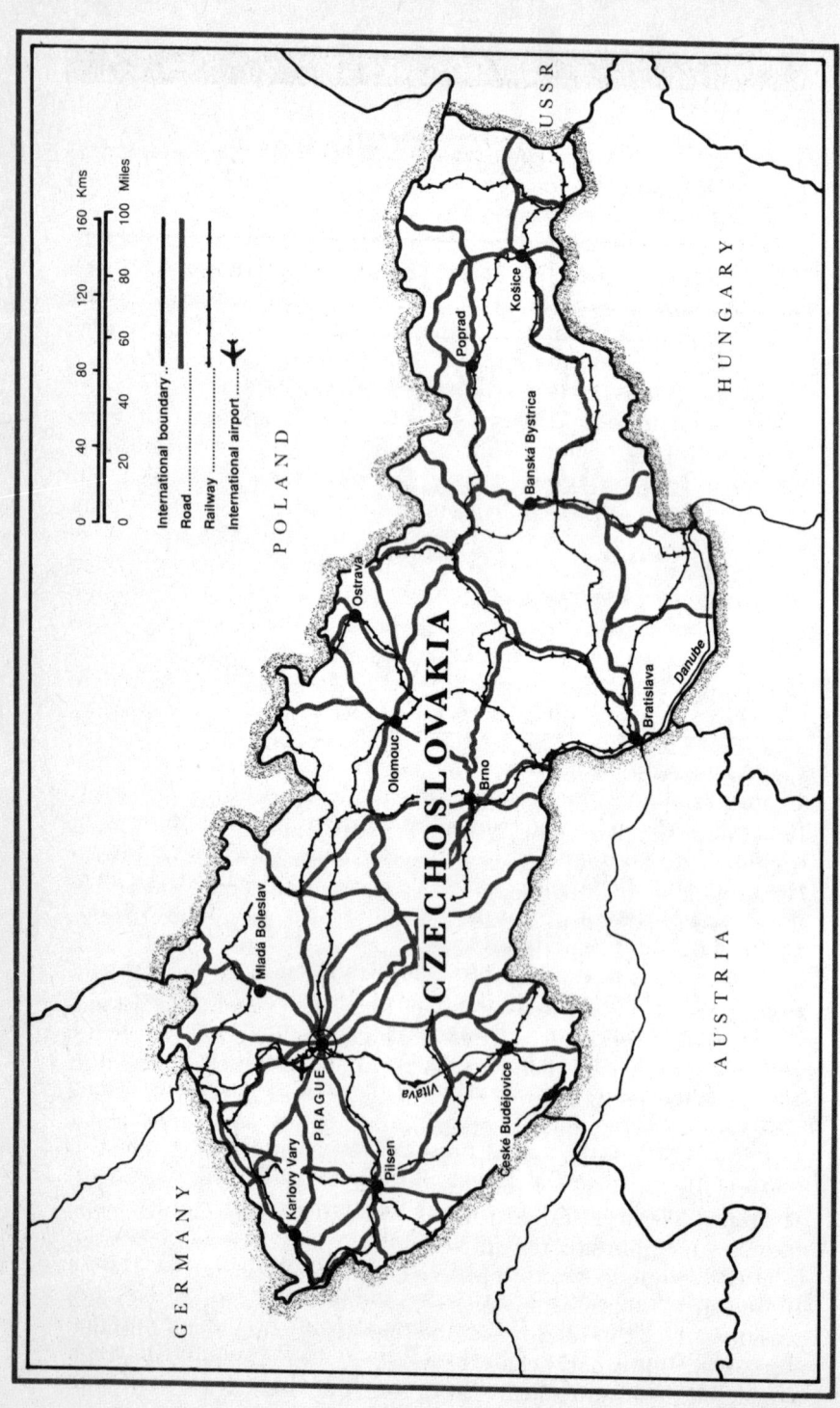

The university was opened, construction of the St Vitus' Cathedral begun, the Charles Bridge was built and some of Prague's architecturally most successful buildings date from this time.

Religious, political and social conflict erupted over the preaching of John Hus, one of the earliest Protestant reformers. Although he was burned as a heretic in 1415, his message successfully combined with nationalism under the new Hussite king, George Podiebrady. It was only under the Habsburgs that the Catholics, led by the Jesuits, returned to power in the 1560s .

However, tension between the Catholic rulers and the Protestant members of the nobility remained. On 23 May 1618, in what came to be known as the Defenestration of Prague, the representatives of the Bohemian Estates threw two Habsburg envoys and their secretary unceremoniously out of a window in the Hradčany Castle. In spite of falling some 50 feet, they landed on top of several centuries of domestic refuse and survived, though unimpressed by their treatment. The Estates then went on to elect a Protestant king, to the great displeasure of the Habsburgs, who saw Bohemia as their personal property. These events triggered off the Thirty Years' War, during which Protestants fought Catholics, and sometimes each other, and in which everyone in Central Europe was involved.

With the annihilation of the Bohemian Estates by the Catholic League at the Battle of White Mountain in 1620 the Czechs became a subservient nation. Even the language was suppressed, being spoken only by peasants and servants, while the ruling classes were obliged to speak German. It was only under Maria Theresa (1740–1780) that Czech could again be taught, and it was the mid nineteenth century before Czech national consciousness was finally revived. Even then, in spite of the efforts of Czech nationalists such as František Palacky, the Czech language was still not considered equal to German. It was only in 1881 that the Czech national theatre was opened in Prague. However, events such as this and the splitting of the university into separate German and Czech entities increased the gulf within the country.

With the outbreak of the First World War, Czech exiles such as Tomas Masaryk, Edvard Beneš and Milan Stefanik seized the chance to emphasise the importance of a strong Slav bloc in Central Europe to counterbalance German influence. At the end of the war, Czechoslovakia was created and Masaryk was elected president. Until 1918 Slovakia too had lived under the Habsburg monarchy, but it had been considered part of Hungary, with the Slovak language and culture suppressed in favour of Magyar. The

Slovaks feared that in joining forces with the Czechs they would merely exchange one oppressor for another, but these doubts were overridden. A reluctant Slovakia and a hostile German-speaking Sudetenland fell within the country's borders, providing Hitler with a convenient excuse to reclaim the land. In 1938 Britain gave in to German pressure, and Czechoslovakia was annexed.

Immediately after the war nearly 3 million German-speaking people were expelled from the Sudeten area of Czechoslovakia where their families had been established for many centuries and were forced to emigrate to their supposed Fatherland. Czechoslovakia was reconstituted, minus its most easterly province which became part of the Soviet Union. In 1948 the Communists took power in a bloodless coup. Although there was initial support for communism, the Stalinist nature of the regime soon alienated many. Twenty years later the uprising known as the Prague Spring took place under a government headed by Alexander Dubček, which attempted to institute 'socialism with a human face'. In August 1968 this was crushed by Soviet tanks, and Czechoslovakia remained part of the Warsaw Pact.

On 17 November 1989, two weeks after the breaching of the Berlin Wall, a demonstration was held to protest against the communist regime. The demonstrators then decided to march on to Wenceslas Square, the traditional centre for important demonstrations. There they were beaten up by the police. From then on events unrolled rapidly, so much so that the Czechs can boast that where Poland had taken ten years and Hungary ten months, they needed only ten days to bring down the Communist government. Students and actors played a leading role in organising strikes and demonstrations. On 19 November, Civic Forum, a loose grouping of dissidents, was established under the leadership of the playwright Václav Havel. Just over a month later, at the end of December 1989, Dubček was elected chairman of the Federal Assembly, and Havel president.

Much has already been written, and much more will doubtless be written, about the 'velvet revolution', whereby a playwright led his nation, as they stood on Wenceslas Square in the snow demanding a different future, to the sound of thousands of keys being rattled. Some of the idealism has since rubbed off as the Czechoslovaks have become more familiar with a pluralist political system. Civic Forum, initially a loose federation of everything that was not communist, and which claimed to be 'a political service', not a party, rapidly developed from a movement of dissidents into a 'proper' political force.

Within two months of the revolution, over forty political parties had registered their formation, indicating their intention to campaign in the elections which were to be held under a system of proportional representation. Each republic – Czech (Bohemia/Moravia) and Slovak – has a national government which deals with agriculture, finances and industry on a local level. The federal government then meets in Prague and deals with similar matters as well as foreign policy, this time at a national level. The federal Parliament has two houses – the lower 150–seat House of the People (101 from the Czech republic, 49 from Slovakia) and the upper 150–seat House of the Nations (75 from each). Each 'nation' also votes for its own assembly. The new parties included the Liberals, the Peasants, the Greens, the Slovakian sister to Civic Forum known as Public Against Violence (PAV), the Christian Democrats and the Communists, whose membership had crashed from 1.7 million in 1989 to only 300,000 by February 1990.

Tensions still remain between the Czechs and the Slovaks, exemplified by a seemingly ridiculous dispute in April 1990 over whether there should be a hyphen between the words 'Czecho' and 'Slovakia'. Eventually a compromise was reached whereby it was decided that the country would officially be known as the Czech and Slovak Federated Republic. However, the deeper nationalist divisions continue to fester, with frequent complaints by the Slovaks that their interests are being subordinated to Czech policies, and increasingly aggressive claims for independence.

The run-up to the June 1990 elections was marred not only by Prague's first terrorist attempt – a bomb planted in one of the main squares, supposedly by disaffected communists – but also by accusations that leading figures had been members of the hated secret police. In the elections, Civic Forum and Public Against Violence won 47% of the vote, followed by the Communists with a surprising 14%, and the Christian Democrats with 12%. The nationalist parties (Moravian and Silesian autonomists, and the Slovak National party) got 15 seats, while the remaining 5 seats went to an alliance of other minorities. Civic Forum's initial concern was to form a broad-based coalition which would enable it to carry through radical economic reforms during the two-year life of the government. Marian Calfa, a former communist, was elected prime minister, with Civic Forum holding the posts of foreign minister (Jiří Dienstbier), finance minister (Václav Klaus) and labour minister (Petr Miller).

ARTS AND CULTURE

In a country where a playwright can be elected president, the arts have a special relevance, and Czechoslovakia has a rich heritage, whether in music (Smetana, Dvořak, Jánacek, Martinů), architecture (from Peter Parler in the fourteenth century, through the baroque master Dietzenhofer, to the art nouveau of Jan Kotera), film (Jan Svankmajer, Jiří Trnka, or the exiled Miloš Forman, director of *One Flew Over The Cuckoo's Nest* and *Amadeus*) or literature. Franz Kafka, who died in 1924, represented the Jewish-German intelligentsia which was wiped out during the war. His most famous works, *The Trial* and *The Metamorphosis*, are bleak and frightening, and have ensured that his name has become synonymous with a particular kind of nightmare. Another early twentieth-century literary figure whose name has entered national consciousness is *The Good Soldier Schweik*. In the novel by Jaroslav Hasek, Schweik is an apparently naive Czech soldier drafted into the Austro-Hungarian army. He represents popular common sense faced with a social and administrative system which oppresses him, and he has become a symbol of the trials of the Czech people.

Today, after decades of suppression, prison or exile, Czechoslovakia's writers are again becoming known and appreciated in foreign translations. While President Havel's plays are now seen in London's West End theatres, authors such as Ludvík Vaculík and Ivan Klíma are gaining recognition. Exiles such as Josef Škvorecký or Milan Kundera, whose novel *The Unbearable Lightness of Being* was made into a successful film, are now free to return.

INTERNATIONAL RELATIONS AND FOREIGN TRADE

The foreign minister, Jiří Dienstbier, summed up his country's international relations in the past by saying, 'Czechoslovakia has been an iceberg in the centre of Europe.' This is not strictly true since, although Czechoslovakia had few Western contacts, it was locked into the Warsaw Pact and Comecon.

As old alliances dissolved, Czechoslovakia began to look hopefully towards the West. It is now very positive about its relationship with Western organisations such as the International Monetary Fund and the European Community. Within a month of the 'velvet revolution' Czechoslovakia had applied to join the International Monetary Fund and the World Bank, as well as the

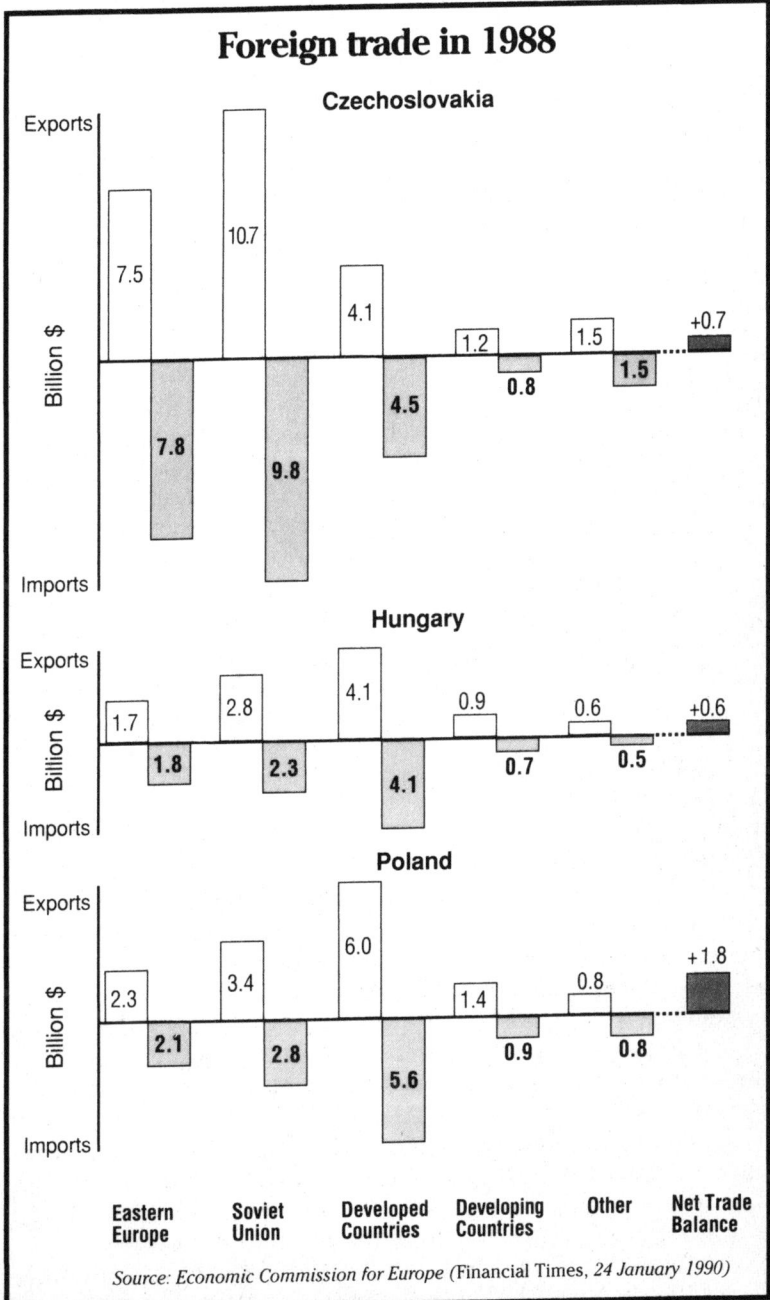

Foreign trade in 1988

Czechoslovakia

Exports

Billion $

7.5

10.7

4.1

1.2

1.5

+0.7

7.8

9.8

4.5

0.8

1.5

Imports

Hungary

Exports

Billion $

1.7

2.8

4.1

0.9

0.6

+0.6

1.8

2.3

4.1

0.7

0.5

Imports

Poland

Exports

Billion $

2.3

3.4

6.0

1.4

0.8

+1.8

2.1

2.8

5.6

0.9

0.8

Imports

Eastern Europe | Soviet Union | Developed Countries | Developing Countries | Other | Net Trade Balance

Source: Economic Commission for Europe (Financial Times, *24 January 1990*)

Council of Europe. With its excellent reputation for repayments, and a comparatively small foreign debt, Czechoslovakia was readily accepted into the international economic community and signed its entry agreement with the IMF in September 1990. The amount of foreign debt used to be a closely guarded secret, but was revealed by the new government to be around $8 billion, falling to $7.1 billion by mid 1990, the lowest per capita in Eastern Europe (apart from Romania, which claimed to have repaid its debts in the last months of Ceaușescu's rule).

Most of Czechoslovakia's foreign exports are in machinery and transport equipment, raw materials, industrial consumer goods, foodstuffs, chemicals and metals. Imports include machinery, raw materials, fuels, industrial and consumer goods and food. In recent years Czechoslovakia ran up only small trade surpluses or deficits with non-socialist countries, a picture borne out by official statistics for 1988, with exports and imports roughly balanced ($24.94 billion exports; $24.26 billion imports). As part of Comecon and the Warsaw Pact, Czechoslovakia traded heavily with other Eastern Bloc countries, with the Soviet Union by far its largest partner. In 1986, for example, nearly 80% of its trade was with other Comecon countries. By 1989 this had fallen to 61.7%, while Western countries accounted for 31% and developing countries for the remaining 7.3% of foreign trade. The Soviet Union's share of trade as in 1988 made up 30% of the total, while trade with Poland, Austria and West Germany rose markedly through 1989.

From past business, the Soviet trade debt in early 1990 stood at some $2 billion in favour of the Czechs, but trade figures for 1990 showed a drop in trade between the two countries of 20%. The Soviet Union proposed a conversion rate to transform their rouble debts into dollars, but there was a dispute about which rate should be applied. The Soviet Union, however, retained a trump card in that Czechoslovakia was dependent on it for oil supplies. Meanwhile, the change from convertible rouble to hard currency accounting should prevent future disputes of this nature.

The greatest increase in trade in recent years was seen with the countries belonging to the Organisation for Economic Co-operation and Development (OECD). Of these, West Germany, as it was then, took the lion's share, followed by Yugoslavia, Austria, Italy, Switzerland, the United Kingdom and France. The shift in trading patterns resulted in an overall growth, though this had slowed by 1989 after two years of solid increase.

A potentially interesting development is the Pentagonale initiative, whereby Czechoslovakia, Hungary, Austria, Yugoslavia and

Italy have agreed to co-operate in regional economic schemes. Launched in Italy in August 1990 it remains to be seen whether it will become an important force.

In February 1990 Czechoslovakia was awarded temporary 'most-favoured nation status' by the United States, and this is expected to be retained on a permanent basis. Czechoslovakia's main exports to the US are textiles, glassware, costume jewellery, clothes, footwear and tractors. It imports spare parts and leather.

The United Kingdom operates very few restrictions against Czech products, although some goods remain subject to the EC Multi-Fibre Agreement (MFA) and the Voluntary Restraint Arrangements (VRAs) for steel and leather footwear. According to UK Department of Trade figures, British exports totalled £131 million and imports £155 million in 1989. Over the second half of the 1980s there was a steady increase in the value of bilateral trade, although the UK share of the market remained less than 2%. Exports from the UK remained unchanged, while imports rose slightly. Early 1990 saw slight increases in both areas.

The UK's top exports in 1989 to Czechoslovakia were: office machines and automatic data-processing equipment; machinery specialised for particular industries; textiles, yarn and fabrics. The top imports were: road vehicles, i.e. Škoda; cork and wood; textile, yarn and fabrics.

In January 1990 Czechoslovakia told the EC that it would not be needing charity in the form of grants and cheap loans, but this was perhaps a little premature. Czechoslovakia and the EC signed a ten-year trade agreement ensuring closer co-operation in all sectors from agriculture to environmental protection. The EC also promised to review leniently the quantitative restrictions (QRs) applied to imports from State trading countries. In July 1990 the EC asked member states to remove most quotas on Czechoslovak goods entering the Community.

Czechoslovakia's new European policy was explained in April 1990 by the then minister of foreign trade, Andrej Barcak, who said the EC was the key marketing area for the Czechoslovak export business. He added that the country's intention was clear: it desired a 'certain form of association' with the present European Community[1]. The EC has enough on its plate at the moment without accepting members with as unclear an economic situation as Czechoslovakia. Nevertheless, influential Czech businessmen tend to talk of 'when we join the EC', not 'if'. Likewise West European businessmen contemplating investment are starting to think in terms of EC regulations, especially for those who may be investing in heavy industry where pollution levels, for instance, are no longer acceptable within the Community.

INDUSTRY

As the Czechs proudly remind critics, they have an impressive industrial heritage. In 1938, they say, their industrial base put Czechoslovakia among Europe's top five countries. During the post-war decades Czechoslovakia invested heavily in steel, mining and heavy industry, and it is currently a leading producer in these fields. In steel, for instance, by the late 1980s it was producing a huge 15 million tonnes a year, nearly one tonne per capita. Around Prague there are many heavy engineering, rolling stock and air-craft factories. The Brno region specialises in engineering works and textiles, Bratislava houses the petrochemical industry, Ostrava in the north is the centre of the coal mining and steel industries, while Pilsen is world famous for its breweries.

Czechoslovakia's erstwhile pride and joy, Škoda, is Eastern Europe's biggest engineering company, with power engineering factories, and other units making everything from cars to rolling mills and locomotives. In mid 1990, Škoda employed 75,000 people, nearly half of whom worked in the power engineering sector. The company produced its first car in 1905, and at the time of the 'velvet revolution', made 100,000 Favorit cars a year, at its factory at Mlada Boleslav north-east of Prague. Over 50,000 of these were exported to the West, with the UK as the biggest market taking over 13,000 each year, and Denmark 7,000.

These industries are very energy intensive, and Czechoslovakia consumes three times as much energy per capita as the rest of Western Europe. It is heavily dependent on Soviet supplies of oil and gas, in spite of turning increasingly to coal and nuclear energy after the oil crisis of 1979. In July 1990, just before Iraq invaded Kuwait, the Soviet Union cut oil supplies to Czecho-slovakia by millions of tons, doubling petrol prices and leading to rationing. The alternative nuclear policy is highly expensive and controversial, especially since President Havel had in earlier life signed petitions against the use of nuclear power. In mid 1990 inspectors found serious safety faults in several of the Soviet-designed nuclear reactors. Austria in particular is increasingly concerned since one of the most suspect nuclear power stations, Bohunice, is only 70km from Vienna. Given the soaring cost of oil, however, the Czechoslovak government has few options in the search for energy sources.

Earlier attempts at modernising the country's industrial structure all proved unsuccessful. By the early 1980s it was evident that the Prague planners had overreached themselves, and thousands of projects remained unfinished. A slight liberalisation was conceded, but there was no incentive or investment for modernisation and industry suffered accordingly. Another attempt at restructuring industry was made in the late eighties. In 1987, for example, several companies were given an experimental degree of autonomy to see if they could become successfully 'self-accountable'. Meanwhile an overall 'reconstruction' was carried out, but to little avail. According to the deputy minister responsible at the time, its failure could be laid at the door of the middle-level bureaucracy, which had refused to implement the 1980 attempts at modernisation. Industrial output fell, and only light industry output rose. The main problems, however, remained the non-competitiveness of the huge state monopolies and the central role of the State Planning Commission, which decided everything from strategy to operational details. In the words of a report from the British embassy in Prague in early 1990, 'Czech industry is now poorly organised, obsolescent, wasteful of energy, and uncompetitive in a large number of sectors.'

Industry faces huge problems, and any reforms may well run into the same obstacles as earlier attempts if middle management and workers are unconvinced of the need to change. However, the spectre of future unemployment looms for many workers and the real possibility of bankruptcy should sharpen motivation.

Economic tensions in the Soviet Union and the pace of East-West *détente* led to a slashing of machinery orders, especially those intended for the military sector. Since some 1.2 million Czechs are directly or indirectly employed in the machinery industry, and much of the product is unsaleable in the West, this is of crucial importance and could result in the loss of over 100,000 jobs. Altogether, the end of the Cold War has proved to be harmful to large sectors of Czechoslovak industry. Apart from the infamous explosive export, Semtex, Czechoslovakia produces tanks and military hardware. It was decided, for instance, that production of T72 tanks was to cease by the end of 1990, with redundancy likely for many of the workforce. Conversion from military to civilian production is likely to affect at least one hundred enterprises in Czechoslovakia and hundreds of thousands of workers.

The mining industry also faces massive unemployment. The north Bohemian mines in Most, for instance, cut 1,000 jobs in April 1990 when it was decided to mine only to customers' actual orders. It was also decided to counter recession by attempting diversification into boiler production and housing construction, and by exporting engineering expertise. Kladno coal mines, just west of Prague, planned initially to close four mines, resulting in the loss of 2,700 jobs out of its workforce of 17,000. Several mines in the Ostrava region were threatened with closure under plans which were released in August 1990.

Steel and engineering are other areas where cuts became inevitable as Czech industry tried to reorientate from heavy engineering towards consumer goods. The Poldi steel works planned to lose 1,500 jobs out of 20,000, and that was only in initial restructuring. More major plans for the works may affect one in four jobs. High unemployment, especially among organised and militant sectors such as the steel-workers, could lead to social and political unrest, particularly when combined with subsidy cuts and steep price rises. It was estimated in December 1989 by Valtr Komarek, deputy prime minister, that $40,000 would be needed to modernise each job in the country, implying substantial foreign investment or state borrowing, which the government is keen to avoid.

According to Dr Jiří Nemec, then deputy foreign trade minister, speaking in early 1990, the government hoped to de-monopolise the country's industries and eliminate central control. The minister for the State Planning Commission would no longer be responsible for planning, but rather for dismembering the Commission itself. By June 1990 it had already been cut to half the number of departments and staff. More radically, state subsidies to ailing industries were to be phased out.

According to the Federal Statistical Office, industrial production fell by 3.6% in the first three months of 1990. The Czechoslovak Press Agency reported that, 'The decline was partly caused by a fall in production in energy-intensive sectors, a slow rate of conversion of military production and insufficient adjustment of products to the needs of the market.' Labour productivity fell by nearly 2%, but wages rose about 6% in the same period.

As a natural result of the new policies, discussed in greater depth below, many – if not most – industries are starting to look actively for investment, usually from abroad, to enable them to modernise. In general, Czech industries need partners to provide expertise, technology, distribution and marketing costs.

AGRICULTURE

In the past Czechoslovakia did not emphasise its agricultural output, seeing itself rather as a country with a manufacturing and industrial heritage. Nevertheless, agriculture is generally considered one of the most successful areas of the Czech economy, with especially good grain harvests in recent years. The main crops are cereals, potatoes, sugar beet, fruit and vegetables, with livestock and dairy produce also making an important contribution. In 1989 agriculture's share of the National Material Product was 6.9%[2]. The sector employed around 890,000 people, 11% of the workforce (see graph on page 43), with wages generally above average.

During the 1950s the 500,000 private farms which existed before communism were amalgamated into a large-scale state system. The private sector retained only 5% of arable land, but nevertheless produced a disproportionately large share of the country's vegetables, fruit and animals. Some 60% of land was reserved for the co-operative sector which proved relatively successful. These farms were smaller than the state models, but still large, employing a workforce of around 400 each and covering an average of 2,500 hectares. Some of the co-operatives were so successful that they were able to expand into other areas. Slusovice, a co-operative in Moravia, provides the text-book example. It started out in farming, but then moved into production of personal computers. By 1990, agriculture accounted for only 14% of its income.

Food shortages, as experienced in Poland and the Soviet Union, never occurred in Czechoslovakia. Throughout the 1970s the centrally-fixed price of meat, for example, remained stable, and in October 1987 the farming minister could declare, 'The state of agriculture doesn't worry me.' (*Financial Times*, 9 October 1987.)

Figures for 1989, released by the Czechoslovak Press Agency in April 1990 showed that, despite a 4.6% growth in turnover in food shops, demand was satisfied. One major problem, however, which agricultural businesses face, and which any foreign investor should consider, is that health and safety standards are in many cases not up to Western European levels. On 1 June 1990 the newspaper *Rudé Pravo* carried a scare report on PCB (polychlorinated biphenol) contamination in milk which indicated that 75,000 dairy cows would have to be slaughtered. Another newspaper, *Zemedelske Noviny*, wrote on the same day that substantial percentages of vegetables and cereals – 19% of all potato samples and 18% of fresh vegetables – were contaminated with excess cadmium and nitrates. Such problems are intermeshed with the overall poor ecological situation in parts of Czechoslovakia.

It is not yet known what will happen in the agricultural sector, but that it will change is certain. Farmers whose land was confiscated under the Communists can now apply to have it returned. The state will no longer subsidise unprofitable agricultural ventures, so many are hoping to reform themselves as joint-stock companies. Monopolies are to be broken up. In April 1990, for instance, the state monopoly of the seed trade ended and seven independent enterprises were established. They hope to become joint-stock companies, possibly attracting foreign investment.

In June 1990, even before the elections, a new enterprise called Strom was founded to deal with technical development, trade and marketing for agricultural organisations. According to one of the directors, Vladislav Bednar, Strom hoped to provide 'assistance in fulfilling the capacities for subsidiary production of the agricultural enterprises and tractor stations.'[3] They would offer totally new skills, such as legal training, advertising, market research and marketing back-up to organisations which had never had to deal with such matters under a centrally-planned economy. Moreover, Strom's reps were to work on commission, another new concept. Such developments are likely to become typical of this sector.

ECONOMIC POLICY

Even before the political revolution of November 1989, attempts at economic reform had been made by the government. The previous year the laws governing joint-stock societies had been liberalised, some attempt had been made to democratise companies by encouraging them to elect their own directors, and some companies were allowed to be self-accounting. None of these reforms were very successful, since fear of uncovering non-competitive sectors within industry or commerce remained strong within the government and Communist party. In other words, the *nomenklatura* (people with a vested interest in the communist regime) was afraid to reform itself out of a job.

As soon as the Communist party had fallen, the new government declared its priorities. In a speech to the Federal Assembly on 19 December 1989, reported in *Rudé Pravo*, the prime minister Marian Calfa announced, 'The first task is elections to representative bodies, while the second one is not merely to secure a smooth running of the economy but also to speed up transition towards dynamising economic development.' The debate was opened as to how to achieve these aims. Valtr Komarek, head of the Institute of Forecasting and future deputy prime minister, and a colleague, Václav Klaus, initiated the discussion. Komarek supported breaking up the state monopolies as a first step. Klaus initially supported 'an evolutionary approach' along 'truly liberal' lines.

In the *Financial Times* of 13 December 1989, just after his appointment as finance minister, Klaus wrote, 'We are afraid of the unrestrained reform romanticism of some of our colleagues . . . We oppose any sort of radicalism . . . We start with the assumption that the efficiency-stifling behaviour of economic agents is deeply ingrained and can only gradually recede.' He proposed deregulation and administrative simplification so that government could retreat to a more limited role, 'careful nurturing' of the market to make it more efficient, the 'liquidation' of various economic activities, and restrictive monetary and fiscal measures. He concluded, 'As true liberals we should start with a very heavy dose of monetarist medicine,' but conceded that while economic performance deteriorated some kind of social contract would be necessary. He did appreciate that there would be many plant closures, but saw it as a very gradual kind of shock therapy. 'We should do it like a television series, an episode every week,' he enthused in the *Daily Telegraph* a few weeks later. His wholehearted commitment to Friedmanite measures was summed up in his cry for 'a market economy without any adjectives,' (*The Economist*, 10 February 1990). His first official act as finance minister was to put in an application for Czechoslovakia to join the International Monetary Fund.

Economic measures came thick and fast in January and February 1990 with laws on taxation, foreign exchange and banking. The monopoly banking system was replaced with a Western-style two-tier structure. A decree was issued creating a bond market. The crown was radically devalued. Laws on private enterprise and joint-stock companies were passed. Andrej Barcak, the ex-communist minister for foreign trade, exclaimed, 'The whole country must become a free-trading zone!' (*Financial Times*, 25 January 1990). Planning commissioner Vladimir Dlouhy announced, 'We will show that we are serious about protecting foreign participation, serious about the right to repatriate profits, serious about moving to convertibility of the currency and about giving all basic assurances required to foreign investors.'

Initially the population supported the reforms almost wholeheartedly. A poll carried out two months after the revolution revealed that 88% of Czechoslovaks thought other developed countries were ten to fifteen years ahead in economic efficiency[4]. Nearly 70% approved the transition to a market economy, while less than 10% rejected it totally. Over 50% were prepared to accept high unemployment for a limited period of time, but over 30% were against any kind of unemployment. Twenty-five per cent of all workers feared the loss of their jobs and anticipated difficulty in finding a new one.

By March 1990 the government had approved measures permitting foreign companies to operate under the same conditions as Czechoslovak companies. Klaus presented his budget which, given the elections, left consumer subsidies untouched, but cut wage subsidies (14%), state enterprise subsidies (11%), subsidies to farmers (13%), and government administrative costs (5%). A new office of privatisation was set up under Klaus' protégé, Dusan Triska. These reforms, for the moment, left untouched the fundamental problem of property ownership. The rules governing private enterprise, repatriation of profits and taxation were also unclear, despite new laws on foreign investment. This led *The Economist* to declare in mid April, 'Czechoslovakia, unlike Hungary and Poland, is not yet open for business.'

Under the Communists, Czechoslovakia had one of the smallest private sectors in Eastern Europe. The new government actively supported private enterprise, and in March 1990 laws were passed giving private companies equal rights to state enterprises. By April 1990 the Association of Czechoslovak Entrepreneurs claimed almost 50,000 members in the Czech Republic and another 30,000 in Slovakia.

Meanwhile splits were beginning to show within the Civic Forum government over the speed and method of reform. Should the move to market pricing follow or precede the break-up of state monopolies? While Václav Klaus supported rapid and radical change, Valtr Komarek wanted a slower and more thoughtful process which would avoid the economic hardships which he foresaw would result from an immediate switch to a market economy. Komarek wanted to improve management skills, develop joint ventures and increase exports through state subsidies before letting market forces have a totally free rein. By May 1990 Klaus, who seemed to be on the ascendant, had prepared the way for internal convertibility of the crown by January 1991, whereby citizens could exchange their crowns for hard currency at their local banks. Full convertibility would be achieved 'two days after we have convertible goods' (*Financial Times*, 2 July 1990). Klaus also put forward a two-stage 'stabilisation programme'. Stage 1, running from 1 July 1990, would lay a framework of tax-exemption and grants to revitalise and restructure industry. Stage 2, coming into force on 30 September 1990, would establish a two-year plan to take into account the effects of inflation and price liberalisation. The debate on privatisation was deferred owing to its complexity. By January 1991 all price controls were to be removed.

While all the parties basically accepted these reforms, Karel Dyba, head of the Economics Institute of the Czechoslovakian Academy of Sciences, remarked in an interview with *The Independent*, 7 June 1990, 'No one really understands what it is all about.'

With grumbling in the background from Komarek, who still believed prices should be held stable while the state enterprises lost their monopolies, Klaus then announced that 25 billion crowns ($2 billion) of subsidies per annum were to be cut. This came into force after the elections in July 1990 with immediate effect on the cost of food, fuel and public transport. The prices of 30,000 items rose by an average 25%. Railway fares, fixed since 1945, shot up 100%, bus fares by 30%. The blow was softened by a monthly hand-out of 140 crowns ($11) to each person, and some prices, such as rents, were still held down. The cut in subsidies left a budget surplus of 16.4 billion crowns ($1.3 billion), in contrast to the previous year's 5.1 billion crown deficit, but it was feared that social requirements would eat into this. Further price deregulation took place on 1 January 1991.

Economic results for the first half of 1990 showed a slow-down in most sectors. Industrial output dropped nearly 3%, the volume of construction work fell 5.7%, foreign-trade turnover fell by nearly 6%. In October 1990 the crown was devalued by more than a third against the dollar, and from 1 January 1991 the crown became internally convertible for trade transactions, but not capital transfers.

As with the other Eastern European countries, Czechoslovakia potentially faces huge social problems as the reforms begin to bite. Unlike Poland, Czechoslovakia has a lot to lose. Inflation in the past has been very low – under 5% – but is certain to rise; unemployment was minimal and officially non-existent; food was readily available and cheap. Inevitably people will be laid off as Czechoslovakia shifts its trade with its main partner, the Soviet Union, from roubles to hard currency, as it effectively loses its second largest market, East Germany, and as industry slims down in an effort to achieve competitiveness.

Raising pensions, maternity grants and child benefits, as was done in March 1990, may alleviate some of the effects of price rises, but not for everyone, and alleviation is a poor substitute for a cure. Estimates of the numbers of unemployed to be expected vary. Petr Miller, minister of labour and social affairs, had funds in his 1990 budget for a maximum of 30,000 unemployed, but local analysts fear the numbers could reach one million within two or three years. Unemployment offices opened their doors in August 1990 and by the end of September unemployment was already at 158,464.

INFRASTRUCTURE

Czechoslovakia, in common with its fellow Eastern European countries, has an outdated infrastructure which is already proving inadequate to the demands made on it. The main international airport is Ruzyně, conveniently situated about 15 km from Prague. It was built in the late 1960s and is small and unwelcoming, totally unable to deal with the near doubling of passengers it has seen since the 'velvet revolution'. The number of passengers flying between Vienna and Prague alone surged 150% in the first half of 1990. Plans are under way to rebuild it totally and there is talk of making Prague airport into a huge Central European crossroads. In their dreams the planners talk of replacing Frankfurt in importance. Meanwhile, tiny Ruzyně airport is struggling to accommodate the thousands of tourists and businessmen who are flooding into the country. Gradually provision for travellers is increasing – in April 1990, for instance, a new daily flight aimed at businessmen flying from Prague to Cologne was launched by Lufthansa, and hopefully facilities at the airport itself should soon be improved. The internal picture is more encouraging with a relatively well-developed network of domestic flights.

Travel by road and rail also received insufficient investment in recent years. Railways are now seen as one of the top priorities, with the emphasis apparently to be laid on speed and efficiency. Most roads are single track, and motorways have been insufficiently developed to cope with any further expansion in road traffic. In June 1990 motorway construction was privatised by the government, and a new motorway has been planned between Prague and Nuremberg to cut out the Pilsen bottleneck. One of the projects under consideration involves putting specific sections of the motorway schemes out to tender. This will involve levying tolls, since government investment is unlikely to be sufficient to pay for major development.

NAMES OF NOTE

Marian Calfa   Prime minister. A Slovak, he trained as a business lawyer, and joined the Communist party in 1964.

Charter 77   A dissident group whose members, in 1977, signed a petition asking the government to fulfil its civil rights obligations. It included many of today's leaders.

Jiří Dienstbier   Foreign minister. Fellow dissident with Havel. Previously a high-flying journalist who then spent years as a stoker in between prison spells for his outspokenness.

Vladimir Dlouhy   Economics minister. Worked in the Economic Forecasting Institute before becoming planning commissioner and then minister. Considered a radical, he is closely allied with Václav Klaus.

Alexander Dubček   Chairman of the Federal Assembly. Communist party leader in 1968, when his reformist programme came to an abrupt end with the armed Soviet intervention. Re-instated under Civic Forum, now something of a figurehead.

Václav Havel   President of Czechoslovakia. A well-known playwright, author of political plays such as *The Memorandum* and *Largo Desolato*, and most recently, *Letters to Olga*. Havel was born into a family of Prague entrepreneurs who lost everything in 1948. He worked in a brewery and as a laboratory assistant before signing Charter 77 and becoming one of Czechoslovakia's most outspoken dissidents. He served several prison sentences before leading the country in the revolution of 1989, in which he was swept to power as president on a wave of public acclaim. In July 1990 he was re-elected president.

Václav Klaus   Finance minister, chairman of Civic Forum. An economist by training, he fell from favour under the communist regime and worked as a lowly clerk at the State Bank. Appointed minister in December 1989, Klaus clashed with other members of the government, including Komarek and Havel, mainly over the radical nature of his reforms.

Valtr Komarek   Deputy prime minister. Previously head of the Institute of Forecasting in the Czech Academy of Sciences, Komarek favours a more gradual kind of economic reform, and has clashed frequently with his colleague, Klaus.

Tomas Masaryk   First president and highly respected founder of the independent Czech state in 1918. His son, **Jan**, was foreign minister in 1948 and supposedly committed suicide when the communists took power.

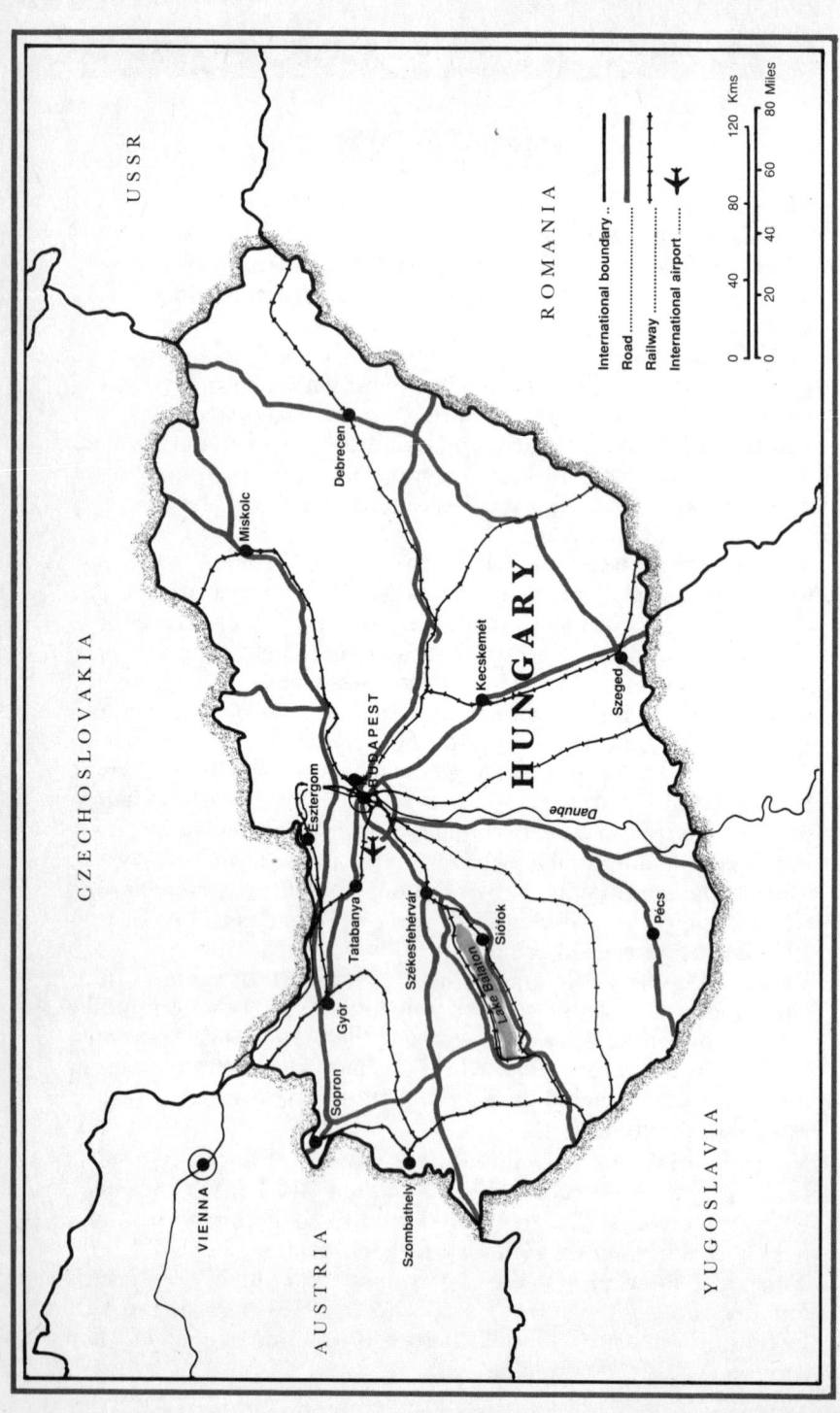

CHAPTER 2

HUNGARY

Official name	*The Republic of Hungary*
Area	*93,030 km²*
Population	*10,300,000*
Capital	*Budapest*
Currency	*forint*

HISTORY, GEOGRAPHY AND POLITICS

Hungary covers about 93,000 square kilometres, most of which is made up of low-lying fertile plain. There are some hills in the north of the country, and one of Europe's largest lakes, Balaton, in the west. The population stands at 10.3 million (1990 census), a decline on previous figures, with 2 million in the capital, Budapest. Sixty-two per cent of the population is urban.

After the fall of the Roman Empire, the province of Pannonia was invaded by many peoples until the arrival in AD 896 of Prince Árpád, leading seven tribes of horsemen down into the fertile Carpathian Basin, a flat grassy plain split in two by the Danube. The legend tells that Árpád sent envoys before him with ornate presents of gold and slaves, requesting in return only a blade of grass and a bottle of Danube water. He so much appreciated the samples which his envoys brought back that the tribes decided to settle, defeating all the local inhabitants, except for the Székely of Transylvania with whom they formed an alliance.

The next landmark date in the history of Hungary is usually given as Christmas AD 1000 when King István (Stephen) was crowned, and embraced Christianity on behalf of his nation, earning himself the title 'patron saint of Hungary'. In 1241 the country was unexpectedly invaded and laid waste by Mongols from the East. This was one of the first and most damaging of many raids which Hungary was to experience in its position on the frontline against the non-Christian hordes of Asia Minor.

During the following centuries the House of Árpád gave way to the French House of Anjou, and Buda, part of modern-day Budapest, became a great cultural centre. The Turks, who succeeded the Mongols as the major threatening force on Europe's eastern flank, were defeated after a century of slow advances in 1456 by the national hero Janos Hunyadi, and his son Matyas Corvinus, the 'Renaissance King', was elected to the throne. After Corvinus' death the Turks attacked once more, and at the famous battle of Mohács in 1526 inflicted a crushing defeat on the Hungarians and their allies. On 10 September 1541 Suleiman's soldiers took Buda. They were to stay for a century and a half.

In 1686 Buda was recaptured by Christian forces, only to become a province of Austria under Habsburg rule. In spite of a happier period under Maria Theresa in the 1740s, Hungarian culture was forcibly Germanised, and in 1848, led by the politician Lajos Kossuth, his rival István Széchenyi, and the poet Sándor Petöfi, a revolution broke out. The uprising was crushed but a compromise was reached whereby Hungary was economically integrated into the Austro-Hungarian Empire under Franz-Joseph.

During the First World War Hungary fought with Germany and Austria until the last days when she broke away under the Communist regime of Béla Kun. The new government fell amidst some bloodshed, and the conservative Admiral Miklós Horthy took over. Under the 1920 Treaty of Trianon, Hungary lost about 50% of her territory to Slovakia and Yugoslavia, while the whole province of Transylvania, the heartland of Magyar culture, was ceded to Romania. The loss of Transylvania still rankles and is a source of great friction between the two countries.

During the Second World War, Hungary again fought with Germany. In 1944 Horthy, still in power, thought better of this policy, but the Nazis immediately occupied Hungary, remaining until its liberation by the Soviet army. Four years later the communists, under Mátyás Rákosi, took over the government. A popular uprising under Imre Nagy in 1956 caused fighting in the streets of Budapest, but Soviet tanks intervened and communist control was re-established. Nagy was executed after a secret trial. The new leader, János Kádár, initially repressed all remaining opposition, but later adopted the famous slogan, 'He who is not against us, is with us,' to justify a relaxation of control. He was able to liberalise the economy slightly, so that by the 1970s

Hungary had become the wealthiest and most relaxed of the Soviet satellites.

In 1988 Kádár was ousted from power, Károly Grosz became General Secretary of the Hungarian Socialist Workers' party, and reformers Imre Pozsgay and Rezsö Nyers entered the Politburo. The unmarked grave of Imre Nagy was rediscovered and, on 16 June 1989, he was reburied with a State funeral in Budapest's Heroes' Square. With Nagy rehabilitated and the Communist regime virtually at an end, Grosz was toppled by more radical reformers, and on 23 October 1989 the new Hungarian Republic was proclaimed and free elections announced.

The populist centre-right Hungarian Democratic Forum (MDF), led by Jozsef Antall, won the March 1990 elections easily with nearly 43% of the vote, 165 seats out of 386. The MDF promoted a lay Catholic, pro-Western but slightly nationalist view. It formed a coalition with the Independent Smallholders party, whose 11% vote was rewarded with four cabinet seats, including the agriculture portfolio, and with the Christian Democratic People's party, who had won 5% of the vote and were given the welfare ministry. The main opposition party was the liberal Alliance of Free Democrats (SzDSz), representing an enlightened urban intelligentsia, with 24%, followed by the ex-communists, now known as the Hungarian Socialist Party with 8.5%. In exchange for supporting the government's constitutional amendments, the Free Democrats' choice of President, writer Árpád Goncz, was nominated. Campaigns at the local elections held in October 1990 were marred by anti-semitic speeches by MDF members. The elections themselves were marked by a low turnout of under 40%, reflecting disillusionment with economic policies, and a slump in the popularity of all existing parties, especially the Smallholders. A few weeks later, petrol price rises of 65% aroused great outcry. The government was forced to back down, raising prices by only 35% and acknowledging that the economic situation was grave enough to be called a crisis.

INTERNATIONAL RELATIONS AND FOREIGN TRADE

Hungary, although the most westward-looking of the Eastern European states, was a member of the Warsaw Pact and of Comecon. It joined the United Nations in 1955 and became a member of a number of international economic organisations in the 1980s, primarily the International Monetary Fund (1982), the International Finance Corporation (1985) and the International Development Association. It is a signatory of the General Agreement on Tariffs and Trades.

Hungary considers itself to be right in the middle of Central Europe. Westwards, its closest links have been with Austria, so much so that the 1995 World Exhibition, Expo 95, was awarded jointly to Vienna and Budapest, in what one of the promoters called 'the first truly Central European exposition,' (*Financial Times*, 25 June 1990). As a result of geographical proximity, and a shared history as part of the Austro-Hungarian empire, Austrian businessmen play a prominent role in the economic life of Hungary.

Relations with the East are less amicable. In 1920 Hungary lost the province of Transylvania to Romania, and has never forgiven or forgotten this. As Ceauşescu's policies of 'systematising' the villages unfolded during the late 1980s, Hungary became increasingly vocal about the problems faced by the Magyar minority in Romania. Refugees flooded across the frontier and Hungarian television made much of their plight. On 27 July 1988, some 40,000 people demonstrated in the streets of Budapest against Ceauşescu's policies, and it was a Hungarian-speaking pastor who sparked off the revolution which swept the Romanian dictator from power. For the present, tension between the countries has died down as the new governments tentatively feel their way, but for Hungarians, Transylvania is a strongly emotive subject which could easily be exploited if the situation worsened.

One of the key events in 1989's year of revolutions occurred in May when Hungary began to dismantle the barbed-wire fence, part of the Iron Curtain, which separated it from Austria. By August, 5,000 East Germans a week were flooding across the border, with thousands more keeping up the pressure by camping around the West German embassy in Budapest. On 10 September, border controls were completely lifted and within 72 hours 12,000 East Germans had left. Within two weeks East Germany's revolution proper had begun, with mass demonstrations leading eventually to the fall of the Communist government. Hungary therefore played a catalytic role in the toppling of communist power in the rest of Eastern Europe, and was keen to underline this crucial fact as Western attention shifted towards Czechoslovakia and Romania.

In November 1989 Hungary applied to join the Council of Europe, the first step perhaps towards applying for membership

of the European Community. As Gabor Brodi of the Hungarian
Embassy in London commented, 'The ultimate goal of Hungary
is to be a member of the European Community. We know that
this won't happen overnight.'[1] In December the Commission
announced a £660 million loan to help the country overcome its
balance of payment problems. This was an extraordinary pre-
cedent at the time, but stringent conditions were imposed. In
return, Hungary was to carry out a reform programme which
would open the way for a free market, end monopolies, reduce
subsidies, deregulate prices and encourage private enterprise, even
if popular opinion later began to turn against such sweeping
changes. A few days later discriminatory quotas on exports to the
EC were also lifted. Hungary initially hoped to obtain membership
of the European Community by 1995, but this is doubtless unrealistic.

Hungary has always had a 'split personality', on the one hand
dealing competitively with the West in hard currency, on the
other bartering in transferable roubles with the Soviet Union. In
June 1990 the Soviet Union claimed that Hungary owed it the
equivalent of $1.5 billion, while Hungary thought it had built up
a massive surplus over the years. Meanwhile, like Czechoslovakia,
the country is dependent on its large neighbour for oil, gas and
other raw materials. The USSR was traditionally Hungary's most
important trading partner, and 41% of exports and 43% of
imports in 1988 were carried out in roubles within Comecon
countries, with another 10% in convertible currency. Imports
from the rouble areas, however, fell by 11% during 1989, and
plummeted during 1990, leaving 71% of all Hungary's trade with
the West, while only 29% was with traditional trading partners
in the East.

In January 1990 licences for exports to the rouble areas were
suspended, and the 1990 economic programme envisaged a drastic
cut of 1.5 billion roubles (approximately $3 billion, at official
exchange rates) in the non-convertible trade balance. In retaliation the Soviets introduced a permit procedure for import of
Hungarian machines and equipment. These measures primarily
affected the engineering industry, whose products were destined
for Soviet markets, with the Ministry of Industry initially esti-
mating that 100,000 jobs could be lost. It was feared that the
collapse of Comecon would cause an initial trade deficit of $1
billion as Hungary struggled to switch its trade westwards. While
the Soviets exported their oil, gas and other raw materials,
Hungary sent back goods which in many cases would have no

purchaser on an open market in the West. Hardest hit would be any company like Ikarus buses which traded directly with the Soviet Union. The Soviet Union could probably sell at least 70% of its raw materials on the open market which, without a substantial increase in quality, could not be said for Hungary's products. As engineering exports fall it seems likely that they will be replaced by exports of food, light industrial and consumer goods.

The squeeze on rouble exports was combined with import liberalisation, altering Hungary's trading conditions radically. CoCom also relaxed its rulings on export of technology to Hungary in June 1990. The country is still trying to come to terms with these changes; shifting the country's whole trading focus from East to West, or even from roubles to dollars is not something that can be achieved overnight. Predictions indicate that exports to Comecon countries will halve between 1990 and 1993. Meanwhile the rise in the price of oil as a result of Iraq's invasion of Kuwait caused terrible problems for Hungary. Estimates as to how much the rise would increase the 1990 budget hovered around the $1.5 billion mark. Every $1 rise in the oil price per barrel is thought to cost Hungary $40 million a year.

Hungary has balance of payments difficulties and its economy is heavily dependent on foreign trade (see graph on page 23). With its high foreign debt and limited natural resources, it desperately needs to increase hard currency exports. Of OECD exporters to Hungary, Germany leads the way, followed by Austria, Italy and then the United Kingdom. Hungary's main exports to the UK include foodstuffs (vegetables and fruit), clothing, electrical machinery and furniture, while its main imports are chemical materials and products, office machines and automatic data processors, textiles, industrial machinery and scientific instruments[2]. Exports to Britain in the first six months of 1990 rose 6% to $8.5 million, while imports fell 10% to $81.4 million.

INDUSTRY

Hungary's geographical situation and natural resources could have been considered more favourable to the development of agriculture than industry, but nevertheless substantial industrial development took place under the socialist centrally-planned economy. Within Comecon, Hungary was encouraged to develop its iron and steel works and to develop an oversize chemical and petro-chemical industry. By 1988 nearly 33% of the workforce of

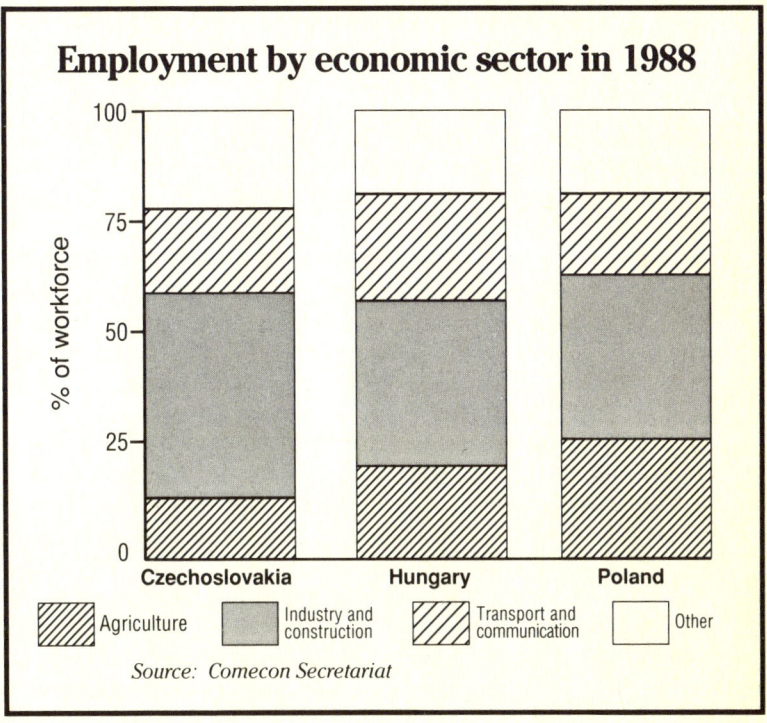

Employment by economic sector in 1988

% of workforce

Czechoslovakia   Hungary   Poland

Agriculture   Industry and construction   Transport and communication   Other

Source: Comecon Secretariat

4.85 million were employed in industry (*Eurobusiness*, May 1990) and 49% of national income was earned through this sector. Hungary is short of fuel and its deposits of oil, natural gas, brown coal and bauxite are insufficient for domestic energy requirements. Most industrial regions are situated around the coal and ore mines, along the Danube, or in the Budapest area, which although declining over recent years, still employ about a fifth of all industrial workers.

The two most important sectors of industry are engineering and chemicals. Miskolc, the historical seat of the country's iron works in the north-east, is the second largest city in Hungary with a population of over 200,000. Even before the recent political changes restructuring was causing problems in the mining and metallurgical companies in the vicinity, and now with its investments in armament production and outdated heavy engineering, Miskolc faces severe problems. In an interview with the *Sunday Telegraph* on 25 March 1990, Karoly Fazekas of the Hungarian Academy's Institute of Economics admitted, 'We know that Miskolc's heavy industries are unprofitable, but because of hidden subsidies and artificial prices, it's impossible to say how unprofitable. Let's just say there's going to be a lot more unemployment.'

In general terms, output from state industrial companies was stagnating or declining through the mid and late 1980s. In 1989, for instance, output was down by over 3% on the previous year. By mid 1990 it was down nearly 8% on the year before. In some specialised cases, such as arms manufacture, orders fell by as much as 30%. Textile output dropped nearly 9% in the same period[3].

Under the Comecon system of distributing different specialities to the member countries, Hungary had become a major producer of buses, mainly through the Ikarus enterprise. The rouble export restrictions imposed in early 1990 caused terrible problems for Ikarus, and resulted in a frantic search for hard currency contracts. Ikarus had been considered relatively successful in switching from roubles to dollars, increasing its hard currency exports from $23 million in 1989 to over $100 million in 1990[4]. Nevertheless, in June 1990 the enterprise initiated bankruptcy proceedings against itself, blaming the restrictions in export to the Soviet market. Of the usual 6,000 buses it sent each year to the Soviet Union, it had exported just 750 when the embargo came into force. Ten thousand workers were laid off. Les Bonnay of the consultancy and accounting firm Price Waterhouse noted in *The European* in May 1990, 'The lay-offs are not due to lack of demand but because the Soviets can't afford to pay. The old system has disappeared but nothing else has been put in its place.' Ikarus assured itself of a recovery as soon as hard currency accounting was introduced, but the government was forced to bail it out, and in October 1990, as production ground to a halt, Western companies were invited to tender to create a life-saving joint venture.

The 1990 squeeze on the rouble trade affected all industries which traded with the Soviet Union. Hunslet, a Leeds railway firm, bought a majority holding in Ganz, a portion of Ganz-Mavag, a huge state-owned conglomerate whose subsidies had been withdrawn prior to the enterprise being parcelled up and sold in sections. A few months after the purchase, just as the new British management was beginning to get to grips with all the problems involved in restructuring the factory, rouble payments were converted into dollars. Harry Codd, the chief executive brought in to run the firm, suddenly found himself faced with the additional worries of organising counter-trade to make up for the shortage of hard currency. Ganz, in common with other state-owned enterprises, had also saddled itself with contracts with other

Comecon countries which were simply not profitable to fulfil. Moreover, it had run up bad debts with other industrial suppliers, but since all were state owned at the time, this had not been considered a major problem under the previous system. Some of these only came to light after the purchase had been completed, and the company accounts were revealed to be of limited reliability. Nevertheless, Codd expected to be making a modest profit from the locomotive works within one year.

Meanwhile Western businessmen are constantly being offered new industrial projects in which to invest. Heavy tomes are issued by the Ministry of Industry listing 'Companies planning for Foreign Capital Involvement', and these give an idea of the breadth of Hungarian industrial involvement. The listing ranges through everything from factories making power stations, through nitrogen works to shoe manufacturers. One hosiery factory offers, among other contributions, 'to utilize its intellectual capabilities better,' in return for supplying 'skilled and relatively cheap labour; an increase of the quantity of marketable products; fast following of fashion trends; product mix extension by product exchange; joint business transactions in third markets and in new geographical locations.'

AGRICULTURE

As the legendary tale of Árpád indicates, Hungary is a fertile country where agriculture accounts for nearly 20% of national income. Two-thirds of the country's area lies within the great Central European plain, producing predominantly wheat and maize, while another 18% is covered in forest. The climatic variety is such that while western Hungary contains pine forests and chestnut trees, southern Hungary and the Balaton area produce wine and figs. Other important crops are fruit (peaches, apricots, apples and grapes) and vegetables (the ubiquitous peppers and tomatoes). Unlike industry, 'the productivity of Hungarian agriculture grew at a distinctly rapid rate and has reached a high standard'[5].

Over 20% of the country's labour force is employed in agriculture, while 16% of total industrial output is devoted to the food-processing industry (see graph on page 43). The agricultural market was until now divided between state farms, co-operatives and small producers. Until the recent political reforms, co-operative farms accounted for just over half of the country's agricultural land, a fall from earlier years. Some 10% of the 1,300 co-operatives were unprofitable, mainly due to management problems[6], but others proved highly successful, as demonstrated by crop yields and other output statistics. The state farms, on the other hand, performed poorly. Both co-operatives and state farms also became involved in other areas such as manufacturing and construction, which may also account for the relative importance (in terms of productivity) of small farms. These covered only 11.6% of total cultivated acreage, but delivered nearly a third of agricultural products. By 1988 state subsidies had been reduced and price controls partially lifted in an effort to make Hungarian agriculture more responsive to the market. Under the post-communist Antall government elected in 1990, it was proposed that over half the nation's land should be reprivatised.

Agricultural products account for a significant proportion of convertible currency earnings. In recent years, however, drought, flooding, frost, depression of international prices and recent rises in feed, fertiliser and energy costs have combined with the cumulative effect of lack of modernisation of equipment to cut into profits. Nevertheless, agriculture remains one of Hungary's most promising areas with good natural resources and potential improvements if attention can be given to areas such as technology, marketing, credit supply and processing.

ECONOMIC POLICY

Hungary, unlike most of the other Eastern Bloc countries, had never fully accepted the principle of a truly centralised economy. As early as 1957, a series of measures had been adopted which slightly liberalised the system. In 1968 a New Economic Mechanism, promoted by Rezsö Nyers, introduced the principle of profit as opposed to output targets. While a centralised economy continued to predominate, co-operatives and some small private businesses were allowed to co-exist, especially in agricultural sectors. The late 1960s and early 1970s were later to be regarded as something of a Golden Age in Hungary's economy, but by 1976 the growth was being financed by a rapidly growing hard currency foreign debt.

Both in agriculture and in small businesses, dynamic growth occurred partly through people taking on a second job and working extra hours. In the late 1980s it was estimated in a survey by Financial Research Ltd that as many as 70% of men were spreading their services in this fashion. The working day had therefore stretched from 8.5 hours in 1976 to 14.5 hours ten years later. The concomitant rise in heart attacks, increased death rate and fall in life expectancy was apparently largely to be blamed on this pressure of work. In 1982 the laws governing small enterprises were further relaxed, and within three years perhaps as much as 18% of the national income was derived from the private sector, an impressive figure for a communist economy. In 1988 plans were laid to give preferential loans to private businesses, and private companies were given legal equality with state enterprises. A year later, as communism was crumbling, a National Association of Entrepreneurs (known as VOSZ) was created, and Hungary soon had the largest private sector in Eastern Europe. By the end of 1990 small private businesses accounted for over 10% of total industrial output, and in some sectors, such as the building industry, the proportion was much higher.

Despite a more liberal economic past than the rest of the Eastern Bloc, by the mid 1980s Hungary's economy, with its industrial structure essentially unchanged, was in serious trouble – 'clinically dead', according to the Central Committee Secretary for Economic Affairs[7]. Western bankers and the IMF (which Hungary had just joined) came to the rescue, but popular expectations had been raised by increased contact with the West, and the Thirteenth Party Congress of 1985 sought to spark off an economic revival. Unfortunately the reforms adopted were only cosmetic, and economic indicators continued to decline while the foreign debt continued to rise. Industrial output for 1985 dropped 1% – it had been meant to rise 3%; the payments deficit for 1986 was $1.4 billion – it should have been a $200 million surplus, and so on. Price increases and new taxes followed, and increased popular discontent. Inflation hovered around 20%, the proportion of the population considered to be below the poverty level grew from one- to two-fifths, with young people and pensioners especially vulnerable. In 1988 journalist Paul Lendvai wrote, 'Rampant corruption, increasing alcoholism, a suicide rate which is the world's highest and sharpening social tensions are a few of the signs of a failed social and economic policy.' That there had not been more hardship was perhaps due to the vigour of the black market which was estimated at a huge 100 billion forints (approximately $1.7 billion) in 1986[8]. In September 1987, János Kádár admitted some responsibility for the economic crisis, and within months he had been replaced by Károly Grosz.

During Grosz's short period in power efforts were made to reform the economy and attract Western investment. In October 1988, for instance, the new company law was passed guaranteeing the legal equality of private businesses with state enterprises. Private stock companies could employ up to 500 workers, instead of the previous 30, and could be founded with a minimum capitalisation of 10 million forints ($170,000). Limited companies required an investment of 1 million forints ($17,000). Three months later the foreign investment laws were liberalised to allow foreign companies 100% ownership. Unprofitable companies, however, continued to be subsidised by the state, and the drastic and unpopular decisions which were considered necessary to salvage the economy were postponed.

Negotiations with the IMF during late 1989 and early 1990 centred on several measures which the IMF considered imperative to ensure Hungary's revival, but it was becoming clear that the economic reforms might give rise to social tensions. Although Hungary had joined the IMF years earlier, inaccurate figures about the level of its foreign debt and failure to meet earlier targets meant negotiations were protracted. The measures prescribed by the IMF included reducing Hungary's current account deficit ($1.4 billion for 1989), devaluing the forint again, this time by 40% (it was devalued three times during 1989), raising interest rates, cutting state subsidies and increasing prices. By now Hungary's foreign debt stood at $20.7 billion, a total concealed by previous governments. This was the highest per capita debt in Eastern Europe and imposed an intolerable burden on the economy. Meanwhile convertible currency flooded out of the country as Hungarians went on shopping sprees to Austria with their new passports, and spent about $1.5 billion within a few weeks. Stringent controls on private currency were hastily imposed.

The budget passed in December 1989 by the caretaker government attempted to take the IMF recommendations on board. State subsidies were cut on everything from food to postal rates and electricity, raising prices by around 25%. Rents were set to rise by 35%, sewage and water by a huge 336% and so on. Although it was still seen as a compromise in some quarters, the budget was described by the finance minister as 'very, very tough'. With inflation at an official 20% (but unofficially perhaps as high as 30%) and the withdrawal of subsidies, families began to find it difficult to make ends meet. Public demonstrations ensued and Budapest saw its first ever public transport strike. The government, however, was encouraged when its current account for the first half of 1990 showed a remarkable $200 million surplus.

The coalition government which was elected in March 1990

was committed to economic reform. Social benefits were raised, but already by March 1990 it was estimated that 2 million people were already living below the social minimum of 5,000 forints (about $80) per month. Initially, the new finance minister, Ferenc Rabár, previously a research economist at the Karl Marx University, decided to take a cautious line, fearing that too hasty a liberalisation would result in foreigners mopping up investment bargains. 'The creation of the infrastructure and the institutions necessary for a market economy takes time,' announced his policy paper published in May 1990 (*Financial Times*, 18 May 1990).

The opening of the Budapest stock market the following month boosted prestige, and the government eventually announced a policy of rapid privatisation which would affect approximately 40,000 small companies (see Chapter 5). Bankruptcy proceedings would be initiated against thirty large state companies, while another 600 were to be 'decentralised'. Small and medium enterprises – 'the motor of the Hungarian economy' – were to be encouraged. Subsidies for exported agricultural products were cut, and prices of luxuries and energy were raised again. The aim was to achieve net savings of 25 billion forints ($375 million) to meet the IMF's target of a 10 billion forint ($150 million) deficit.

As a result of Hungary's history of economic progressiveness over the past decades, the government's progress towards creating the legislative framework for investment, and the slightly more advanced infrastructure necessary to support a market economy, Hungary has been seen by the international business community as being the most accessible country in Eastern Europe. A survey of large multinational companies, carried out in September 1990 by DRT International, placed Hungary well in advance of its neighbours.

The social costs of these economic policies, however, are expected to be very high. Visible signs of social discontent took some time to reveal themselves. Street demonstrations were sparked off by the January 1990 price rises, miners went on strike in July 1990, but the government hastily made concessions on pensions and pay claims, and the matter was resolved within the week. In 1987, unemployment was still known as 'retraining', since it officially did not exist, but by the last day of 1989 it was reported as being 7,873 or 0.17% of the working population of 4.5 million. By mid 1990 unemployment began to rise sharply, hitting 61,000 by October. It is expected to continue to rise sharply and the Employment Fund's budget was increased three-fold in preparation. Meanwhile, inflation also rose and by September

1990 it was running at an official 27%. The government was facing widespread and public disillusionment.

INFRASTRUCTURE

Hungary has a great deal in common with its Eastern neighbours, unfortunately including an underdeveloped infrastructure.

Railways are under particular pressure. MAV, the national railway system, claimed in mid 1990 that it was facing bankruptcy and was unlikely to make any profit for the year. Fares were raised as convertibility became accepted, especially for international fares to other Comecon countries, and MAV pinned its hopes on World Bank assistance.

Roads suffered during the 1980s from cut-backs in the construction and maintenance budgets, which in turn led to a marked deterioration in quality. According to a survey carried out by the highway authorities and published in May 1990, there were only 200 km of motorway in Hungary. Thirty per cent of roads were 'of good quality', another 12% had 'a good surface'. In 1989, however, nearly 30% less resurfacing was carried out and consequently the roads need substantial attention. Some foreign credit, including World Bank loans, was available. The 2 million cars driving around Hungary have an average age of nine years and nearly 30% have two-stroke engines, causing unnecessary pollution.

Within the capital, Budapest public transport authorities claimed that ageing vehicles, worn tramlines and substantial fare increases (87% in early 1989 for instance) were ruining the system. Nevertheless, for someone used to London transport, the system seems to run efficiently. A joint venture with a French company, Matra, is to provide the 'transport system technology' for Budapest's fourth underground railway, a link with the new World Exhibition site on Csepel Island, to be ready for 1995[9].

Altogether the exhibition, Expo 95, requires massive foreign capital to create the infrastructure needed for Budapest to cope with a major influx of foreign businessmen and tourists. The authorities estimate that thousands of millions of forints will be needed to supply road and rail links, hotels, campsites and cultural programmes. There is currently a shortage of hotel space, and during international fairs it is difficult to find a room.

The international airport, Ferihegy (I and II) is 19 km from Budapest. It hopes to become an international crossroads, and several airlines, such as Singapore Airlines and El Al, opened offices in Budapest during 1990 in anticipation of increasing demand. Austrian Airlines reported a growth of 21% in the number of passengers on its Vienna to Budapest flights. There are currently plans under way to open subsidiary airports throughout Hungary. Siofok near Balaton, Szombathely near the Austrian border and the ex-military airfield at Tokol near Budapest have been suggested as sites. A US-Israeli construction company has also been considering a project to build an international airport in eastern Hungary to relieve pressure on Frankfurt as a central European crossroads[10].

Telephones are another major problem. Hungary has one of the lowest ratios of telephones per person – 15 per 100 people, according to 1988 data, although it is far higher within Budapest itself, which has 47% of the country's telephone lines, but only 20% of the population. There are half a million people on the waiting list for a new telephone, and it is thought that millions more would register if they thought there was any chance of success. Average waiting time is twelve years, unless the engineers' hearts are softened by a few thousand dollars in the hand. Getting an office with more than one line into it can be considered a major achievement. One British businessman, crammed with his staff into an office the size of a small cupboard, gloated, 'I'm not moving. I've got three lines here!' The loss to the economy caused by this inefficient system is estimated at millions of forints.

There are plans to invest $6–7 billion over the next ten years, and the World Bank has offered credit. Over the next three years 520,000 new lines are to be installed. Foreign businesses see this as a crucial area, and as the government de-monopolises the sector, breaking the Hungarian Postal Administration's monopoly, several companies are already moving in. Early in 1990 an Austro-Canadian-Hungarian joint venture was eyeing BHG, one of the largest telecom-equipment manufacturers, while an American-Swedish-Hungarian company was bidding for the cellular telephone market. Within five years, Hungary's telephone problems should be alleviated, if not completely solved.

In the meantime courier companies have moved in. DHL opened offices in Budapest and Györ, and was planning more. TNT formed a joint venture with Malév, the Hungarian airline. Both reported favourably on the volume of business in the first few months.

NAMES OF NOTE

Peter Akos Bod   Minister of industry and trade. Cosmopolitan expert of the Hungarian Democratic Forum. Previously visiting lecturer at several American universities.

Jozsef Antall   Prime minister. Democratic Forum, ex-director of the Museum of Medical History.

Árpád Goncz   President. Alliance of Free Democrats. Writer and translator who spent six years in prison under the communist regime.

Károly Grosz   General Secretary of the Communist party, 1988–89.

Béla Kadar   Minister of international economic relations. Former director of the National Planning Institute, where he researched Hungarian foreign trade.

János Kádár   Communist party leader, 1956–1988.

János Kis   Leader of the Alliance of Free Democrats. Philosopher.

Imre Nagy   Leader of the 1956 uprising. Executed at a secret trial, but rehabilitated and reburied in 1989.

Ferenc Rabár   Finance minister during 1990. Non-party. Ex-research economist at the Karl Marx University, then with the State Planning Office.

CHAPTER 3

POLAND

Official name	*The Republic of Poland*
Area	*312,685 km²*
Population	*38,210,000*
Capital	*Warsaw*
Currency	*zloty*

HISTORY, GEOGRAPHY AND POLITICS

Poland, with a population of 38 million, is Europe's seventh largest country. On the north it is bordered by the Baltic and on the south by several mountain ranges (Sudeten, Tatra and Carpathians) which mark the boundary with Czechoslovakia. The highest peak is Rysy at 2499 metres. Some 60% of the population live in cities, with 1.6 million in the capital, Warsaw, which is at the geographical centre of the country, on a huge flat plain. The east and west frontiers have less of a natural geographical line and have been the subject of many battles throughout the centuries.

Poland was first united as a state around 960 AD under the Piast prince, Mieszko, who was the first ruler to convert to Christianity. A short-sighted system of inheritance weakened the ruling family, so much so that the Teutonic Knights, who had been invited in to help Christianise the country in the early thirteenth century, were encouraged to take possession of northern Poland. The natives of Gdańsk were massacred and the town was renamed Danzig and repopulated by German colonists. Even in 1990 the 'Danzig corridor' remained a sensitive issue between Poles and Germans during the negotiations over German reunification.

After attacks on the eastern frontier by Tatars, King Kazimierz the Great managed to unite the country again in 1333. This resulted in a peaceful interlude, but the Teutonic Knights were

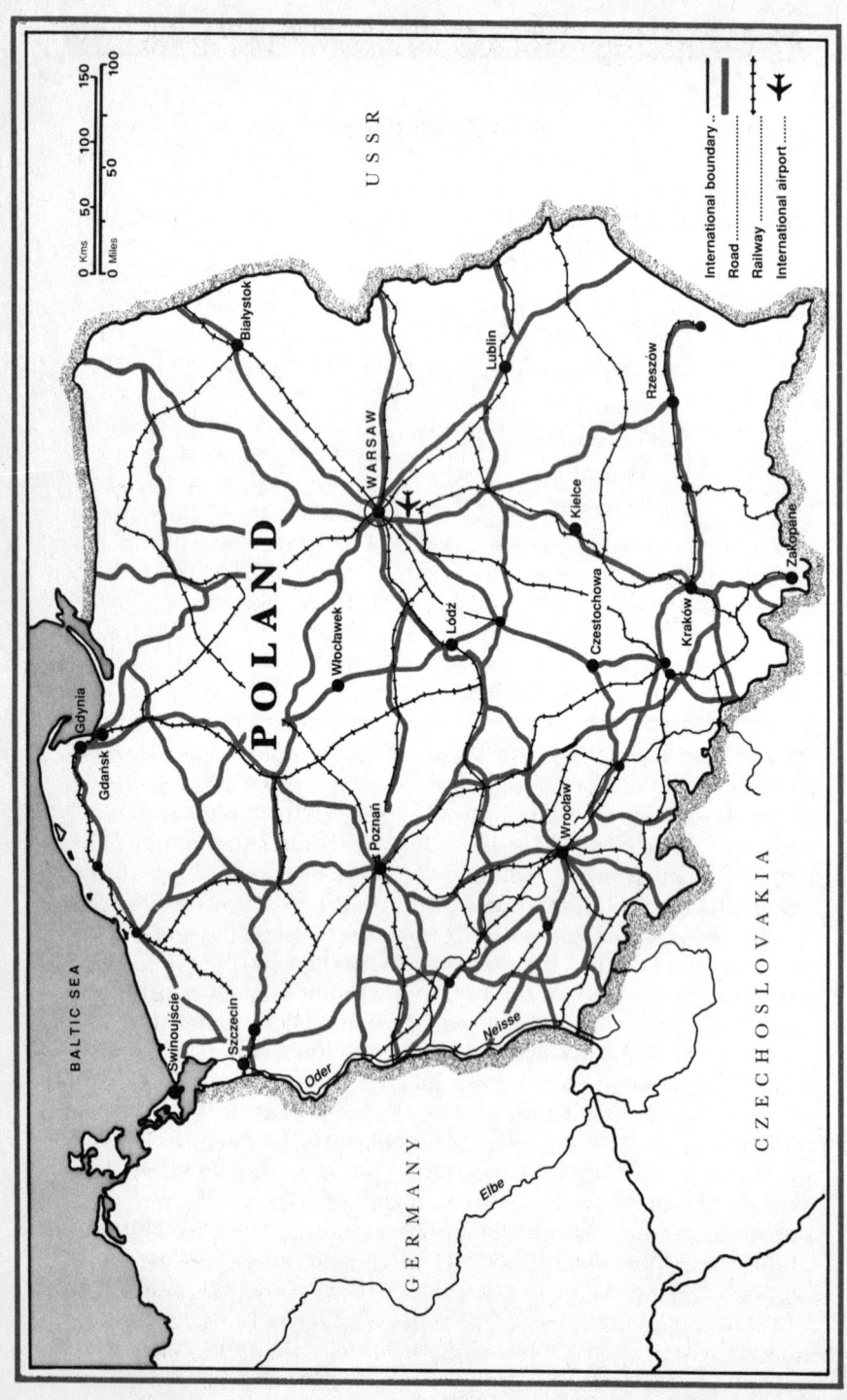

not decisively defeated until the mid-fifteenth century.

The sixteenth century was Poland's Golden Age which produced many artists and scientists of note. In 1573, however, the ruling Jagiellonian dynasty became extinct and the Parliament or *Sejm* (pronounced *same*) adopted a new constitution which abolished hereditary monarchy and adopted elective kingship. This disastrous policy led to factionalisation among the Polish nobles and several weak foreign kings were elected to the throne, culminating in 1655 in an invasion by the Swedes under their Vasa rulers.

In spite of the achievements of King Jan Sobieski, who defeated the Turks outside Vienna at the end of the seventeenth century, in 1772 Poland was in such a state of disorganisation that Austria, Prussia and Russia were able to annex nearly 30% of the country in what came to be known as the First Partition. For national historians, the Parliament's greatest achievement was the liberal Constitution of Third May 1791. The French-Revolutionary tone of this document worried Catherine the Great of Russia and, with Prussia's aid, she carried out the Second Partition, this time devouring more than half the remaining territory of Poland. Tadeusz Kosciuszko led a rebellion against the Partition, but was defeated. In 1795 the Third Partition between Russia, Prussia and Austria swallowed the rest of Poland. The country had ceased to exist.

Insurrections against foreign rule occurred throughout the nineteenth century (notably in 1830 and 1863), and the figure of the desperate Polish patriot became something of a cliché in European courts. In the end, though, it was only in 1923, as a result of the Treaty of Versailles and with the help of armed conflict on several frontiers, that Poland was resurrected as a nation.

Barely sixteen years later, on 1 September 1939 Nazi Germany invaded Poland, thereby initiating World War II; within five weeks the country had succumbed. Poland lost a higher proportion of its population than any other nation – 20%, or over 6 million people. Its 3 million Jews were sent to concentration camps, its universities were closed, its intellectuals murdered, its cities razed. By the time the Red Army liberated Poland at the end of the war, 80% of Warsaw's buildings were destroyed.

Under the post-war settlement, Poland's borders were moved hundreds of kilometres to the west, following the line of the rivers Oder and Neisse. In the process it gained several major cities from Germany, including Szczecin (Stettin in German) and Wrocław (formerly Breslau), while it lost some areas in the east to the Soviet Union, including Wilno and Lwow. Hundreds of thousands of

Germans were expelled from the new territory. A huge work of reconstruction began, and Warsaw was totally rebuilt exactly as before the war. Poland soon found itself in close alliance with its liberators, the Soviet Union, becoming a member of the Warsaw Pact and later Comecon. Wartime devastation – 85% of all industrial plant in ruins, 60% of all railways unfit for use, nearly 100% of bridges destroyed, and 90% of cattle, horses, pigs and sheep slaughtered – encouraged the Poles to follow the Soviet model and introduce a centralised planning and command structure.

In 1978 Bishop Karol Wojtyla of Kraków was elected John Paul II, the first ever Polish Pope. The following year he visited his homeland, drawing huge crowds in the most devoutly Catholic country in Europe. This visit is seen by many as triggering off the events which were to follow. In 1980 strikes in the Baltic ports led to the creation of Solidarity, the independent trade union led by Lech Walesa. In December 1981 General Wojciech Jaruzelski imposed martial law and arrested thousands of Solidarity members. In spite of several amnesties during the 1980s, tension remained. In 1984 a young Catholic priest, Jerzy Popieluszko, became a national martyr when he was murdered by secret police.

Two waves of strikes and the liberalising policies of Mikhail Gorbachev forced the authorities to agree in 1988 to round table talks with Solidarity. The trade union created a political wing, the Civic Parliamentary Club (OKP), and partially free elections were held in June 1989. Ironically Poland then found itself over-taken by events as the rest of Eastern Europe embarked on completely free elections. The system of government was modified to allow for a parliamentary opposition, a president and a two-chamber National Assembly, along with a free electoral system. The upper 100–seat chamber is known as the Senate, and the lower 460–seat chamber as the *Sejm*. The assemblies elect the president for a 6-year term. Each province, or *voivodship*, elects two candidates to the Senate, which can veto or propose changes to the *Sejm's* legislation. Supported by a two-thirds majority, however, the *Sejm* can overturn a Senatorial veto. On a local administrative level, Poland is divided into 49 *voivodships* and over 2,000 rural communities. Considerable power is held by the Civic Committees, ad hoc Solidarity groups which organised local and national support. Constitutional change, however, is being drafted and should be implemented by late 1991.

Solidarity won a resounding victory in the June 1989 elections. Sixty per cent of seats were reserved for the ruling communists, but of the remaining seats Solidarity won an overwhelming 99 out of 100 in the Senate and all the allocated 35% in the Lower House. The Communist party dissolved itself and reformed under two rival Social Democratic banners. After long negotiations, Solidarity was virtually forced to take on the responsibility of government, almost before it was ready. The Communists were offered the Ministries of Defence and the Interior, but while General Jaruzelski remained president, Solidarity nominee, Tadeusz Mazowiecki became prime minister. Walesa remained without an official post within the government, a position which he occupied uncomfortably for some months.

On 30 December 1989 the People's Republic of Poland changed its name back to the Republic of Poland, and replaced the crown on its official emblem, the white eagle.

As discussions on the pace of economic reform continued throughout 1990, two parties within Solidarity began to emerge. In June 1990 the Centre Alliance, considered more populist and right-wing, emerged supporting Walesa and his bid for a strong presidency for himself. An opposing party, the more liberal Democratic Action (abbreviated to the acronym ROAD) supporting the policies of Mazowiecki, was formed a few months later by Solidarity activist Zbigniew Bujak in response to this development. Presidential elections were held in November 1990 and Mazowiecki was forced into a humiliating third place behind Walesa, and an unknown Canadian émigré, Stanislaw Tyminski. The level of support that Tyminski managed to raise through promises of economic improvement indicated the desperation many Poles felt at the grim economic prospects. Polish intellectuals despaired at the lack of political maturity which the results revealed, and anti-Semitic comments and accusations of demagoguery dominated the campaign. Walesa promised that economic reforms would continue on course, with Leszek Balcerowicz, Mazowiecki's finance minister, in charge, though with 'certain corrections'. These corrections were taken to mean greater intervention in factory closures, agricultural subsidies, and a purge of ex-communists. The new prime minister was Jan Krzysztof Bielecki, leader of the Liberal Democratic Congress, a small free-market party.

INTERNATIONAL RELATIONS AND FOREIGN TRADE

The Polish Soviet-style economic plans of the 1960s and 1970s stressed redevelopment and new construction of heavy industry – chemicals, engineering, ship-building, metallurgy. One lasting achievement of the post-war years was the development of the port cities complex of Gdańsk, Sopot and Gdynia, the so-called Troj-miasto region, a development which resulted in a huge increase in cargo handling and ship-building capacity.

The Comecon countries were the main international markets of Poland, and supplying these markets was the main incentive to create large-scale manufacturing of a size far beyond what the home market demanded or could support. Throughout the 1980s, the threat of Soviet retaliation if social and economic liberalisation proceeded too fast kept the brakes on political reform, until the policies of Gorbachev led to the collapse of communism.

While Poland remained a reluctant convert to the policies of its eastern neighbour, relations on the western frontier also provided a source of tension. The Federal Republic of Germany came under considerable pressure from organisations representing the 8 million ethnic Germans who used to live in what is now part of Poland, to leave the question of the Western borders in abeyance. With the reunification of Germany in 1990, however, the West German government grudgingly renounced all territorial claims.

Poland's relations with the outside world over the last decade were generally dogged by debt and seemingly endless negotiations about rescheduling of repayments. The country's sufferings under martial law in the 1980s created a great fund of goodwill in Western Europe and the United States towards the newly emerging Solidarity government, fostered by the substantial Polish exile population. During the 1990 presidential elections, however, some of this fund was dissipated by the overt anti-Semitism which resurfaced. Poland, like Hungary and Czechoslovakia, hopes to join the European Community at some point in the future, although relations with the Community currently revolve around aid. As soon as the Communists relinquished power, the EC extended a generalised system of preferences (GSP) to Poland, and swiftly allocated programmes of aid, predominantly food.

Meanwhile Poland is trying to increase the amount of exports to Western Europe, away from Comecon and the rest of the old socialist bloc (see graph on page 23). Coal and its by-products head the list of Polish exports to Britain. Other major exports include iron, steel, crude fertilisers and unprocessed minerals. Poland's main imports from Britain are general and specialised industrial machinery and equipment, scientific instruments, electronic office equipment and other automatic data-processing equipment.

INDUSTRY

Poland has substantial natural resources. It is amongst the world's largest suppliers of hard and brown coal, and also has large reserves of copper, sulphur, lead, silver, zinc, magnesite, chalk, kaolin, potash and natural gas. The major industries are based on these resources and account for nearly 50% of Poland's Net Material Product. Of this, 16.2% comes from engineering, 7.5% from food processing, 6.8% from mining, fuel and energy, and 6.7% from light industries[1].

Important industrial towns include Lódź (textiles), Kraków and Wrocław (engineering, railways, steel), Poznań (engineering, railways and trade fairs), Gdańsk and Szczecin (shipbuilding) and Katowice (heavy industry, coal, steel, chemicals).

In the 1970s Poland invested over ambitiously in heavy industry, drawing on credits offered by the West. According to George Blazyca, '"gigantomania" gripped and dominated the imagination of the leadership'[2]. This policy left Poland with massive interest repayments, and the subsequent lack of hard currency led to shortages of parts and materials, which in turn caused factory stoppages. Plagued with strikes and faced with the growth of Solidarity, Poland experienced a major economic crisis in the early 1980s.

The rest of the decade saw a slight recovery, but the problems remained acute. Polish efforts were heavily biased towards older energy- and material-intensive industries, such as mining and heavy engineering. Its dependence on coal exports, outdated technology, an unmotivated work-force, short working hours, lack of supplies and a poor infrastructure were firmly tied into the central planning system which was too inflexible to react efficiently. In the mid 1980s some enterprises were declared bankrupt, and 140 large and medium-sized loss-making factories, including the Lenin shipyard in Gdańsk were supposedly targeted for closure[3]. The construction, chemical, engineering, textile, food and metallurgical industries were stagnant or declining. Only the coal, fuel and power industries saw any growth, especially in the Belchatów and Lublin areas. The problems were so serious that even a willing investor like Mrs Barbara Piasecka-Johnson, the Polish-born millionairess, was frightened off when she tried to buy the Gdańsk shipyards in 1989. Workers and management valued the yards at $40 million while Mrs Piasecka-Johnson's accountants thought they were only worth $6 million. The prospective purchase, desperately needed by the yards, became even more

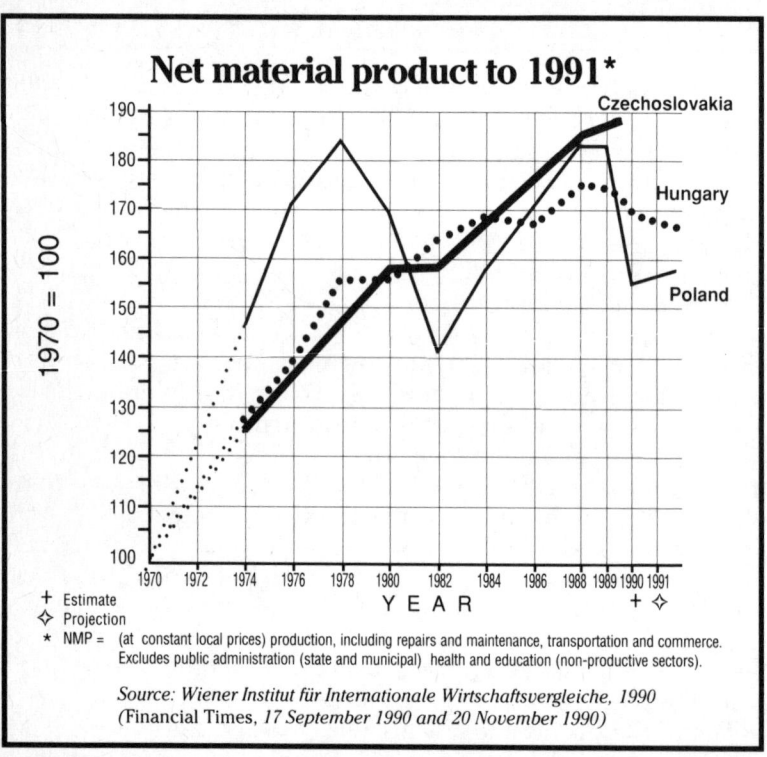

Net material product to 1991*

Source: Wiener Institut für Internationale Wirtschaftsvergleiche, 1990
(Financial Times, *17 September 1990 and 20 November 1990*)

+ Estimate
◇ Projection
* NMP = (at constant local prices) production, including repairs and maintenance, transportation and commerce. Excludes public administration (state and municipal) health and education (non-productive sectors).

unpalatable to Walesa's workers when word leaked out about the number of redundancies the new owner was planning.

Poland is now the leading producer of coal in Europe, and coal, coke and briquettes head the list of its exports to the United Kingdom. In the first quarter of 1990, however, none of Poland's 70 collieries made a profit in spite of receiving almost 10 billion zloties in subsidies[4].

AGRICULTURE

Among Eastern European countries, Polish farmers showed the stiffest resistance to Stalinist collectivisation of their land in the 1950s, so much so that the private sector was permitted not only to continue in existence, but even to exceed state holdings. While the official size limit for private farms was supposed to be 50 hectares, 100 hectare farms were not unknown, although most of

Poland's 3 million peasant proprietors lived off around 15 hectares or less. It was only in 1983 that private farms of any size were finally officially accepted by the government and given the same legal status as the state farms. These small farms were often family holdings, technologically and organisationally underdeveloped, but nevertheless fulfilling a crucial role in supplying Poland's agricultural requirements.

During the crisis of the early 1980s agriculture suffered enormously, as the lack of hard currency and the sanctions ordered by the West as a result of the imposition of martial law led to shortages of fodder and fertilisers. Meanwhile, many people, faced with growing food shortages, started to grow produce on tiny plots of land.

In 1986 agriculture produced nearly 15% of Poland's GNP; of this, private farms supplied 78%[5]. Almost 30% of Poland's total labour force is employed in agriculture (see graph on page 43) and even urban workers often have close peasant family links, with a small allotment cultivated on the outskirts of the town, or several members of the family still based in the village of origin. Under the previous system, land could be handed over to the state in return for an old-age pension, and this resulted in large tracts of land, which should have been available for cultivation, being left fallow.

Poland's main agricultural crops are cereals (predominantly wheat), potatoes, sugar beet and fodder crops. Timber, beef, cattle and pigs are also important sectors. Polish preserves have a world-wide reputation for quality, especially gherkins, strawberries and redcurrants.

The small size of most Polish farms, their lack of mechanisation and technology, poor distribution system, a shortage of spare parts, fodder and fertiliser, and a basic lack of convertible capital, combined with high interest rates, present major problems for Polish agriculture. It is estimated that maybe a third of small farms will have to be sold in the new economic climate. Those farmers who have been able to survive under this system, such as those who since the reforms have managed to sell directly to consumers and cut out the costs of middlemen, will be looking to increase the size of their farms. This could be achieved either by buying up neighbouring holdings or by merging into local co-operatives, and thus spreading the costs of investing in equipment.

During the months of high inflation in late 1989, farmers were accused of hoarding grain to force the price up, and to retain a hedge against inflation. Then, as Western food aid arrived and subsidies on most foodstuffs were slashed in January 1990, farmers were left with unsold produce, and began to demand a minimum state purchasing price to guarantee their income. Prices for state purchases, however, lagged behind inflation, while prices of agricultural machinery and fertilisers rose. Further demands included preferential interest rates on loans and high customs tariffs on imported food. Farmers felt they had been ignored politically, and by June 1990 were dumping lorry-loads of potatoes outside the Ministry of Agriculture to underline their plight. Ludwik Majart, a cabbage farmer and a former member of Solidarity, commented, 'Farmers must have their own party. Our new government is good, but not good for farmers.' The problem for the government was that farmers' demands for price guarantees ran exactly counter to the IMF prescription for curing the economy, and the resignation of the minister of agriculture in July 1990 did nothing to solve the underlying problem.

If immediate difficulties could be resolved, Polish agriculture might turn into a major national asset, with a highly motivated sector supplying much of the country's needs and earning much-needed foreign currency through the export of high-quality food.

ECONOMIC POLICY

Poland's economy has been at crisis point for years. The 1970s legacy of heavy spending and high foreign debt combined with political unrest, military rule and Western sanctions left Poland to the full enjoyment of its centrally-planned and technologically backward economy. In 1971 the foreign debt was $1.2 billion. By 1980 it topped $23.5 billion. The proportion of the nation's exports needed to service the debt rose from 12.4% in 1971 to 83.2% in 1980 (*The Times*, 5 April 1982). This was clearly impossible to sustain and throughout the 1980s talks on debt rescheduling continued, with greater or lesser success.

In 1985 Poland joined the International Monetary Fund. Some reforms were attempted in the early 1980s whereby companies were to become self-financing, and relatively autonomous in terms of company policy. The state was, in theory, to restrict itself to supplying 'economic parameters' within which enterprises should function. The 'Directions of Economic Reform' of 1981, for example, laid emphasis for the first time on profit. The following year legislation was passed permitting companies to be established using foreign capital, as long as the foreign partner was of Polish descent. Over 700 companies, known collectively as 'Polonia', were set up under this system.

A slight recovery was felt from 1983, but Leszek Balcerowicz, the future finance minister, at that time a lecturer at the Central School of Planning and Statistics, noted that in the short term, 'No economic system could produce favourable results here,' and in fact these tentative reforms were effectively torpedoed by the apathy and vested interests of the bureaucracy and the *nomenklatura*.

In 1987 General Jaruzelski's government tried again, restructuring prices, improving conditions for joint-venture partnerships and cutting the number of ministries from twenty-six to a mere nineteen. In 1988, the second stage of reforms was initiated. State and private companies were now to enjoy equal conditions. Wholly-owned foreign subsidiaries were permitted and foreign currency controls were loosened. By 1989 the ruling Communist party was even trying to encourage a market economy, though still trying to maintain full employment and a high level of social and public services.

On his accession to government, the prime minister, Tadeusz Mazowiecki, and his finance minister, Leszek Balcerowicz, faced huge problems. The most pressing was the $39 billion debt, owed mostly to West Germany (20%), France (11%), Austria and Britain (8% each). The second problem was the rampant inflation. In the longer term the debate raged as to how, and how fast, to privatise the state enterprises. Substantial aid was offered by the West Germans, the Americans and the European Community. Lech Walesa went on a tour of foreign capitals and told the United States Congress, 'We seek buyers for 80% of the Polish economy. We can't find them in Poland, because Poles are poor.... In Eastern Europe you can make the business deals of the century. We need Columbuses to go eastwards, who, in the jungles of the East, will create a new legal system, a new business system, a new banking system...' Poland was rewarded with industrial, environmental and food aid. The EC too offered food shipments, money for training, infrastructure and environmental projects. The UK set up a Know-How Fund of £50 million to be spent over five years (see Chapter 6).

Through late 1989 the zloty was repeatedly devalued, virtually every ten days, while inflation continued to soar. In spite of the European Community's food aid (including 5,000 tonnes of olives!) price increases began to cause real hardship among the population. By November 1989 it was established that more than 4 million Poles were on or below the poverty level, while the inflation rate was a staggering 557% per year.

The main negotiations continued meanwhile with the IMF. Eugenio Lari, head of the World Bank's East European operations, estimated that Poland needed around $20 billion over the next three years in terms of debt relief, economic support and new lending. By Christmas 1989 the main package had been decided, opening the way for other loans and rescheduling repayment agreements. In return for a £460 million standby loan, and with another £600 million to follow, the Polish government agreed to reduce public expenditure, control the money supply, cut government subsidies, block wage increases, reform the banking system, liberalise foreign trade, curb central investment and devalue the zloty still further. It was real shock treatment; kill or cure. As Balcerowicz acknowledged, 'The Polish economy is very sick. An operation is needed, a deep surgical cut removing the inflation which is wreaking havoc.'

The new policies came into force on 1 January 1990. Wages were practically frozen until the end of April, and subsidies were cut on most commodities. Coal, heating, transport, electricity and food prices shot up, some as much as 500%. At a stroke, queues disappeared as people suddenly could no longer afford the goods on offer. Traffic jams too vanished as people were forced to leave their cars at home; meat reappeared in the shops after decades of shortages. Unemployment jumped from 9,600 in December 1989 to 55,800 by January 1990, and to 152,000 a month later. A major recession seemed to be setting in as industrial sales for February were announced as being 29% down on the previous year. There was a short strike of miners in Silesia in January and of the railwaymen in May, but in general government popularity initially remained around 80% as people accepted that the severe hardships were necessary in order to achieve a long-term improvement.

To the government's relief and pride, the zloty held firm at around 9,500 to the dollar. February's year-on-year inflation rate peaked at 1,266%, as producers passed increased costs on to their customers, but then demand constraints started to show results and by June inflation was down to about a monthly 4%. By April it was clear that Poland had achieved a near-balanced budget, the abolition of most subsidies, a currency devalued to a sustainable rate and the freeing of 90% of prices. There was even a surprise $800 million trade surplus for the period January to March, the largest for forty years. Foreign debt service obligations were rescheduled until March 1991.

The recession, however, was deeper than expected, at least

according to official figures. Unemployment continued to rise, hitting 500,000, or just under 4% of the workforce after the first six months of the year. By the end of October 1990 it had topped the million mark, reaching 1,008,416, or 7.5% of the workforce, with the eastern part of the country worst hit. Living standards dropped by a third and retail sales for June were 50% down on the previous year.

Industrial sales for the first six months of 1990 still showed a fall of 28.7% compared to the same period in the previous year; light industry and food processing were the hardest hit sectors. Jerzy Osiatynski, head of the Central Planning Office, sadly noted that enterprises were simply adapting passively to the decline in demand[6]. In other words, they were raising prices, rather than improving efficiency. The foreign debt still stood at $40 billion for July 1990.

On the other hand, perhaps as much as a third of retail sales were carried out unrecorded by semi-legal street traders. Throughout the towns of Poland trucks parked at strategic points threw open their back doors and offered everything for sale from vegetables to sugar. Elsewhere car boot sales sold flowers, shoes and rubber piping. Entrepreneurial Poles have become a byword in Berlin, and private enterprise, at least on a small scale, is obviously flourishing. In June 1990 the Polish Press Agency reported that 131,000 new private firms had been created, nearly half of which were 'in commerce.'

Lech Walesa, not happy with what he considered a slow pace of change, began to clash with the prime minister, Mazowiecki. While the foreign debt repayments and inflation were being tackled, long-term policies, on privatisation for instance, had been delayed. The necessary legislation was finally passed by the *Sejm* in July 1990, but the debate on how to divide up state enterprises and how to prevent the ex-communist *nomenklatura* from exploiting the situation, remained to be resolved.

Under pressure from Walesa's Centre Alliance, and faced with rapidly declining living standards, the government decided to shift emphasis. The incomes policy was slightly relaxed. The privatisation campaign was stepped up to concentrate on breaking up state monopolies, and part of the unexpected budget surplus was to be spent on measures designed to alleviate some of the worst effects of the recession. It was not, however, enough to keep Mazowiecki in power, and Walesa was elected president, promising to continue the same economic policy with some unspecified 'corrections'.

INFRASTRUCTURE

Poland has thirteen airports, of which four (Warsaw, Kraków, Poznań and Gdańsk) receive international flights. There is a substantial domestic air network. Most major airlines fly into Warsaw's rather rudimentary airport, Okecie, situated 7 km from Warsaw's city centre. A new terminal built by a German firm with a capacity of 3 million passengers a year is due for completion in 1992. There are also plans to expand Gdańsk airport so that it can handle nearly 1 million passengers a year.

There are 27,000 km of railway track, which in 1988 handled 430 million tons of freight and about 1 billion passengers. In July 1990 the European Investment Bank provided the government with a $30 million low-interest loan to improve the railway service by computerisation and modernisation of stock.

There are over 150,000 km of road, which carry over half the national freight. In 1988, 640 million tons of freight travelled by road. Nevertheless, there are very few motorways, most roads being single track and shared between cars and picturesque horse-drawn carts.

There are four major ports on the Baltic, at Szczecin, Swinoujście, Gdańsk and Gdynia. Gdynia has a container facility, Szczecin is planning to construct a container-handling terminal, and Gdańsk has oil and bulk handling facilities. There is also a reasonable inland water transport network.

The telephone system is in a very poor state (see graph on page 104). Crossed lines are usual and fax machines extremely rare. The Benetton representative for Eastern Europe, herself based in Austria for reasons of efficiency, remarked, 'If you want to call Warsaw, put aside five or six hours.' AT&T are providing a new international exchange; other exchanges are planned, and Siemens formed a joint venture in mid 1990 to make digital public telephone switching systems. Independent networks, used by banks, hotels and other businesses, are to be negotiated as soon as the law forbidding foreign companies to construct telephone networks has been modified.

NAMES OF NOTE

Leszek Balcerowicz   Finance minister since September 1989. Ex-professor of economics, Central School of Planning and Statistics, and economics adviser to Solidarity in its earliest years.

Jan Krzysztlof Bielecki   Walesa's caretaker prime minister since January 1991. Ex-Solidarity economist.

Zbigniew Bujak   Long-time Solidarity activist, organiser of Democratic Action.

Bronislaw Geremek   Ex-chairman of the OKP, Solidarity's group in Parliament. Historian.

General Wojciech Jaruzelski   Former Communist leader. Imposed martial law in 1981, but remained president under Solidarity government until November 1990.

Jacek Kuron   Labour minister. Well-known dissident.

Tadeusz Mazowiecki   Prime minister June 1989–December 1990. Long-time adviser to Solidarity, and ex-journalist.

Adam Michnik   Highly respected editor of the best-selling newspaper *Gazeta Wyborcza*. Supporter of Mazowiecki.

Jeffrey Sachs   Harvard economist, adviser to the Polish government.

Lech Walesa   Leader of Solidarity, 1980–1990. Gdańsk electrician and winner of the Nobel Peace Prize in 1983. 'I don't want to be president. I will have to be president,' he said in July 1990, and was sworn in five months later.

CHAPTER 4

AREAS OF INTEREST FOR THE WEST

There are many sectors in Eastern Europe which look promising for outside investors, in both the short and the long term. Market and profit opportunities combined with cost advantages are tempting for Western investors. Historically, culturally and geographically Eastern Europe has always been part of Europe and it makes sense to see it as part of the greater post-1992 market. However the chronic lack of hard currency is a limiting factor in almost all situations, and the key at present is how to get around this problem. There are five possible solutions:

● The first is to identify products or services which could be sold in the West for hard currency and to use barter or counter-trade to access the market profitably. This is certainly the quickest way to make money out of Eastern Europe, but in practice it is very hard to find or obtain saleable products.

● The second possibility is to supply goods and services which can be paid for in hard currency by Western organisations such as the World Bank or the EC, or even by Western companies who are themselves investing in Eastern Europe.

● The next possible solution involves setting up operations locally which manufacture for export. This involves a much greater investment of time and money, but the number of sectors in which this approach could be tried is almost limitless.

● The fourth solution covers those sectors which can earn hard currency directly, such as tourism, hotels and advertising (for Western companies). These sectors are attractive because they can provide hard currency earnings from day one and are therefore low risk. The problem here is, everyone else realises this, so competition from other Western companies is likely to be intense.

● The final approach to the opportunities in Eastern Europe is a venture capital one: invest money in building operations which do not generate hard-currency profits in the short term, but which will provide very handsome returns in the five- to ten-year time frame upon their sale. Clearly this is not appropriate in every sector and for every investor, but there are many very large opportunities that can only be realised in this way.

Czechoslovakia, Hungary and Poland have different strengths and weaknesses. Hungary is the most advanced in terms of political openness and development, of banking infrastructure, economic attitudes and in terms of the evolution of a legislative framework capable of supporting the return to a free market economy. Czechoslovakia has a skilled labour force, and with its strong engineering tradition, relatively well-managed enterprises, excellent tourist potential and lower national debt, it is in a strong position to attract Western investors. The saying goes that, but for communism, Czechoslovakia would have been like Switzerland. Poland too has its attractions and offers many opportunities. It is one of Europe's largest countries, and with a population almost the size of Spain's, one of its main advantages is the sheer size of its potential market. It also provides a useful half-way stage in accessing the Soviet market.

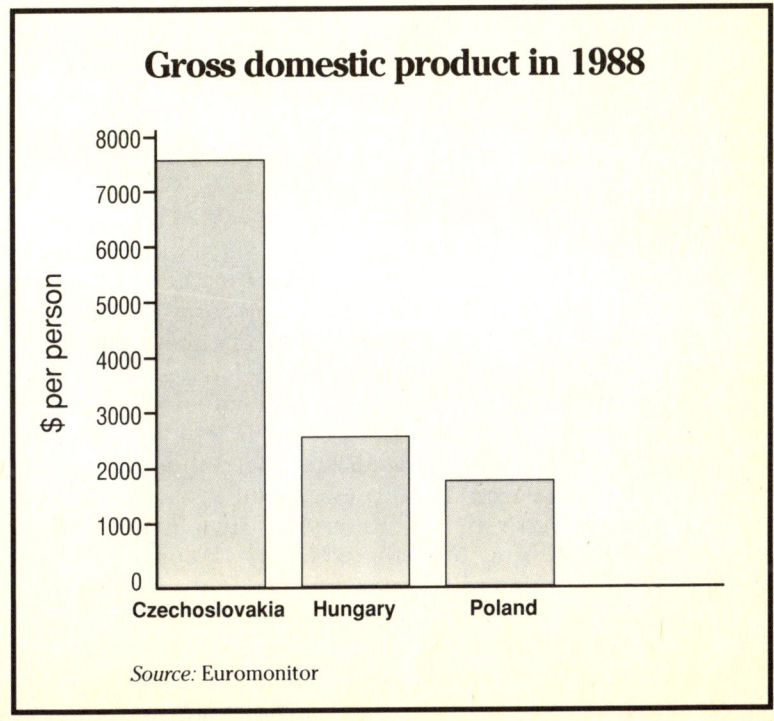

Gross domestic product in 1988

Source: Euromonitor

Nevertheless, the disadvantages cannot be ignored. All three countries, and Poland in particular, suffer from poor transport and communications. Inflation is also a lurking problem, especially in Poland and Hungary. Czechoslovakia lags behind the other countries in terms of legislation, widespread ignorance of the workings of a market economy and currency convertibility. All three are dogged by top-heavy bureaucracies, uncertainty over property ownership and legality of processes, poor technology, underdeveloped private sectors and a lack of entrepreneurial and managerial skills. Each investor must obviously weigh up the pros and cons of his own opportunity, bearing in mind the need to pre-empt the entry into the market of any competitors. The solution may be to make contacts and establish a presence, making the minimum possible investment while waiting for the right moment for a full-scale commitment. The value of such contacts, and the information to be gained from having established an early foothold in Eastern Europe should not be underestimated.

Some areas look particularly attractive and bear closer investigation.

ADVERTISING AND MEDIA

One look at a pre-1990 Eastern Bloc publicity leaflet for any product reveals at a glance the scope in the field of advertising. Quaint phrases and fuzzy, greenish-brown illustrations extol the virtues of the spa waters of Marianské Lázně or the latest 'fashions' from the state textile monopoly. In a society where goods were in short supply, the best advertisement was a queue and a glimpse of fresh tomatoes. Companies had no need for advertising and allocated no specific advertising budget. Apart from political slogans extolling the achievements of the communist way of life, advertising was only thought necessary to find foreign buyers, and this was mostly carried out through the medium of exhibitions and trade fairs. These still remain very important, with as much as two-thirds of advertising expenditure still spent in this area.

Before the opening up of the East, all advertising had to be arranged through selected state enterprises such as Interpress in Budapest, and all forms of media were party controlled. There were long waiting lists to book an advert – an incredible three weeks for daily newspapers, and a six month delay to get an advertisement into a periodical. Advertisers hoping to promote new services and products, especially banking, insurance and new consumer goods, were initially faced with an acute shortage of media in which to advertise. Free advertising broad-sheets soon began to appear in the streets of Budapest and Prague.

Western companies have already been moving in, especially into Hungary where advertising has been permitted since the 1970s. Ogilvy & Mather bought 60% of the largest agency, Mahir, in early 1990. A few months later Young & Rubicam bought into another Hungarian company, Skala, and then cast acquisitive eyes towards Czechoslovakia. In the short term, the populations may lack sufficient funds to purchase the advertised goods, and distribution and production difficulties may cause problems getting the goods to would-be buyers, as was the case when Disco crisps were sold out in Czechoslovakia within two days of the first advertisements. However, all the major international players have realised that the area is too important to ignore.

For some months after free elections in each country, the local newspapers and magazines experienced editorial bliss, freed from the constraints of censorship. Then they began to experience a market squeeze. Jobs and readership were no longer guaranteed,

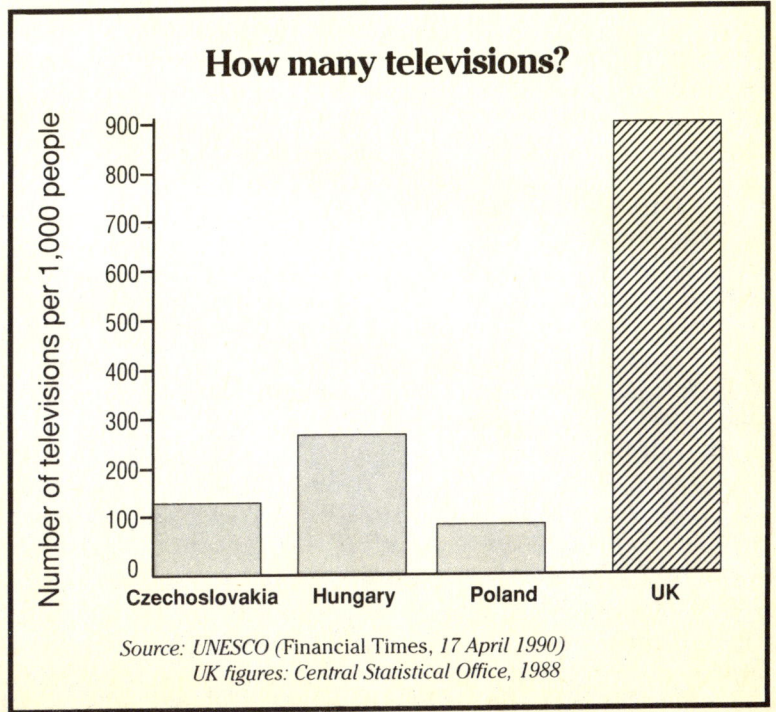

How many televisions?

Source: UNESCO (Financial Times, 17 April 1990)
UK figures: Central Statistical Office, 1988

and more specifically, newsprint had to be paid for at market prices. New technology was desperately needed, here as elsewhere, and job losses occurred. New areas, however, opened up. Soft porn magazines, long restricted and confiscated at the borders, finally became available. The first private television station in the East, in Wrocław in Poland, went on air in February 1990. In Hungary, by July 1990 the Ministry of Transport and Communications had received fifty-six applications for private radio stations and forty-six for television channels. Within a year of semi-free elections, 300 companies had been formed in Poland to deal with communications' services in one form or another, and similar 'studios' abound in Budapest and Prague. The media in general is obviously an attractive proposition. Rupert Murdoch bought shares in the weekly newspaper *Reform* and the daily *Mai Nap*. Robert Maxwell's Mirror Group took shares in the daily *Magyar Hirlap*, while Axel Springer controversially took over the regional newspapers of the Hungarian Socialist party itself.

In general terms, advertising and the media are areas where the Eastern countries are starting virtually from zero. The media was previously repressively state controlled but are now booming. In the short term, shortages of hard currency among both advertisers and buyers may present problems, but in the long term these areas show great potential.

COMPUTERS

In 1989 there were 400,000 computers in Hungary, of which the vast majority belonged to individuals. Thirty-five thousand were used for teaching, and the remainder were used by the state. Demand is huge, and Poland and Czechoslovakia lag behind Hungary, which has many well-respected computer programmers.

In June 1990 CoCom, after pressure from West Germany and France on the United States, eased controls on the sale of vital equipment such as precision machine tools, telecommunications equipment and computers. As a result the CoCom list of controlled categories was trimmed from 116 to 38 items. The relaxation saw an immediate increase in interest from the West. Within a month the West German company AEG opened an office in Katowice to sell its products for automating industrial processes and IBM, already present in Prague, Bratislava and Ostrava, opened in Kosice to help integrate East Slovakian universities into a joint network.

New regulations and legislation, as well as the demands of

industry, helped to stimulate demand. From 1 July 1990, for instance, all receipts issued in Hungary for both retail trade and services were obliged to detail price and VAT. A till with a memory suddenly became a necessity, and Western and Japanese companies moved in to satisfy the demand, with Casio providing tills for assembly by a Budapest co-operative

With all sectors, from industry to individuals, desperate for computers, sales are limited by hard currency rather than demand. ICL, for instance, has gone in for a complex barter system in Poland, exchanging furniture for computers in an effort to get round this problem. One British computer company which exhibited at the Brno Fair in 1989, ROCC Computers Ltd, had within six months signed contracts worth £2.5 million in Czechoslovakia. These sales included orders from Chemopetrol, Centrotex, the Textile Foreign Trade Organisation and Czechoslovak Railways. Ken Kasey, commercial manager for ROCC in Czechoslovakia, which has been dealing in the area since the 1970s, said, 'A lot of people never bothered before, now more are prepared to go in.' Not only is there more competition from Western business, but the Czech market has suddenly become more complex as it decentralises and splits up. 'On the face of it, it looks better now, but underneath it's chaos,' Kasey said. 'It's going to be a long, long time before it all levels out.'

Prompted by the relaxation of CoCom rules and the perceived need for advanced technology, BICC Data Networks signed a contract to supply computer networking systems, initially to Hungary. The deal is expected to be worth £5 million. Phil Mercer, Data Networks' sales and marketing director, explained, 'Hungary was our first choice because it is the most economically and politically developed with an emerging modernised industrial base and growing financial institutions.'

This area shows great potential for growth, especially with the development of new areas, where demand for new technology will be high.

ENVIRONMENT

As Eastern Europe opened its frontiers a scene of appalling pollution was revealed. The concentration on energy-intensive industries, obsessive secrecy and a callous disregard for the health of workers means that Eastern Europe now faces huge environmental problems. Hardly a week passes without another media horror story about pollution in Eastern Europe, but the fact remains that investors must take into account clean-up and modernisation costs, because levels tolerated under an earlier regime are no longer acceptable. The new governments, their neighbours and the EC have expressed anxiety over the levels of pollution.

In the Bratislava area, for instance, air pollution is estimated at fifteen times the official permitted level. The Czechoslovaks use between 70 and 100 million tonnes of highly polluting lignite, resulting in 18 tonnes of sulphur dioxide deposition per square kilometre per year, twice the West German and six times the French rate. If all pollutants are included, it is calculated that about 25 tonnes are pumped out by Czechoslovak industry per square kilometre each year, almost fifty times the Swedish level (*International Herald Tribune*, 5 December 1989). Since its inefficient factories use as much as 40% more energy than the West, it is hardly surprising that Czechoslovakia's forests, especially in the north, are critically ill. The government accepts that it must reduce hard coal and lignite consumption. Seventy percent of Czechoslovak rivers are polluted with mining waste, nitrates and untreated sewage. Life expectancy in most of the country is sixty-eight for men, and seventy-five for women, around five years less than in Western Europe, and in some areas even lower[1]. It is estimated that 90 billion crowns ($7.2 billion) will be needed to achieve ecological balance by the year 2000[2].Although no Greens were elected in June 1990, Civic Forum has promised to attend to ecological issues.

In Hungary, the statistics again make grim reading. The country's air is heavily polluted – it has been estimated that 30% of the air pollution emanates from car exhausts (mainly from the antiquated, obsolete two-stroke engines), 60% from industry and 10% from household heating. Life expectancy is sixty-six years for men and seventy-three for women. Hungarian ecological protest coalesced during the late 1980s around the building of the controversial Gabcikovo-Nagymaros Danube dam, which was shelved in May 1988 amid great uproar after Hungary became the first East European country to appoint an environment minister. By July 1990 the project had already cost the country 33 billion forints ($528 million) and the Austrian constructors were demanding further billions in compensation for the cancellation.

Poland's record on pollution is even worse, and has led to it being dubbed 'the dirtiest country in the world'[3]. The Polish environment minister, Bronislaw Kaminski, called Silesia, 'the most polluted part of Europe.' He acknowledged that at least 100 polluting enterprises would have to be closed down, and that

Poland would need to shift away from heavy industry (*Financial Times*, 18 June 1990). Even the old regime acknowledged the problem, declaring twenty-seven 'ecological danger zones' and five disaster areas. In Upper Silesia and the Kraków region, sulphur dioxide deposits exceed 100 tonnes per square kilometre. The air catches at the throat as one comes into view of the factories, and it is no surprise to find that cancers, throat disease and chronic bronchitis are more prevalent here than in the rest of Europe. Life expectancy is a decade lower than in the West. In the last five years it has fallen from sixty-nine to sixty-four years for men, but in the most polluted part of Southern Poland, only 3% of men live to receive their pensions at sixty-five[4]. Half of Poland's rivers are biologically dead. The Vistula, which flows through Warsaw, is so polluted that even industry cannot use its waters for fear of corroding its piping.

In 1980 the Polski Klub Ekologiczny (PKE) was founded, not surprisingly, in Kraków. Other 'greenish' organisations, such as Wolnosc i Pokój (Freedom and Peace) were also founded during the 1980s, their membership greatly boosted by the accident at Chernobyl, which seriously affected Poland. The most notable achievements of the decade were the closure of the Siechnice steelworks in 1986 and the election of a Green mayor in Kraków in 1989.

The governments of all three countries are aware of the problems they face. They are also aware of the costs involved. The World Bank, for instance, estimated that $25 billion would be needed this decade to bring Polish pollution levels into line with the rest of Europe. In June 1990 the three countries, along with the Soviet Union, decided to participate in the European Environment Agency. The Polish delegate explained that Poland had so far received about $25 million (£14.8 million) of environmental aid from the EC. The Eastern delegates underlined that they hoped for help with training, information and technology.

This is an area where the West can assist the East, and help itself in the process, since pollution knows no national frontiers. Past damage must be cleared up. Factories must be updated to use cleaner technology. Pollution-control equipment, recycling technology, nuclear safety, effluent disposal and water treatment plants are only some of the areas needing attention. Clearly this represents a major opportunity for the Western manufacturers of pollution-control equipment. The question remains, of course, how to satisfy the demand profitably, given the lack of hard currency throughout Eastern Bloc governments and enterprises.

In the area of pollution-control equipment, this problem may be less acute than in other areas of industry. Western governments' response to the environmental disaster in Eastern Europe will include an increasing amount of financial aid linked to the purchase of Western pollution-control equipment and services. One approach to this market will therefore be to help Eastern Bloc governments and enterprises present their cases for financial aid for pollution control to organisations such as the World Bank or the European Bank for Reconstruction and Development.

Much of the cost of reducing the East's pollution will also be borne by Western companies who have acquired Eastern manufacturing facilities. Another way to approach the Eastern market for pollution-control equipment is therefore to market to the Western acquirers of polluting manufacturers. A final approach would be to supply equipment in exchange for a stake in the East European companies helped.

ACCOUNTANCY, MANAGEMENT CONSULTANCY AND MANAGEMENT TRAINING

'Qualified Accountants. Eastern European Languages.' In 1990 such advertisements started to appear in the press as accountancy firms began to realise the potential of the new market.

In the words of *Accountancy*, the journal of the Institute of Chartered Accountants, writing in February 1990, 'In the absence of a market economy it is quite impossible to prepare meaningful accounts.' The first thing any would-be Western investor is likely to do is to ask to see the company accounts. The lack of useful information gained in their perusal is just another stumbling block which the East can ill afford to put in the path of any potential investor. Hence their enthusiasm for Western accountants, and the invitation from the Polish and Czech authorities requesting Western aid in this sector. The Institute of Chartered Accountants set up an East European Task Force under Ian McFarlane in March 1990 to help re-establish professional accounting bodies with Western-style standards.

Moore Stephens International was the first British accountancy firm to get a licence to perform audit work in Poland. Chairman Gervase Hubbert considered setting up the Warsaw office as a long-term investment. 'It is definitely not for the faint-hearted,' he commented (*Accountancy*, February 1990). Since then all the large companies – KPMG, Price Waterhouse, Coopers & Lybrand Deloitte, Ernst & Young – have moved into Eastern Europe *en masse*.

Not only accountancy, but also its sister skill, management consultancy, was in such short supply in communist Eastern Europe as to be unknown. As the countries try to drag their industries into profitability, there is an unprecedented need for high-level expertise in management and financial fields. The main restraints, as usual, are how to pay the consultants, given the lack of hard currency, and a certain ignorance of their role within a company. However, with the desperate need for advice on Western methods, there is little of the resentment which calling in external consultancies can provoke in the rest of Europe. One way around the payment problem is to work for one of the international aid agencies who have earmarked funds for the payment of consultants. Another way is to operate in both directions – as advisors to Western companies seeking entry to an unfamiliar area, and as advisors to Eastern companies seeking information on restructuring and attracting capital.

Almost all Eastern European companies are keen to send their staff to the West for training, in search of the elusive panacea, management skills. The offer of a period abroad, working with Western management and equipment, familiarisation courses or help with setting up accounting methods, are important factors for enterprises looking for, or choosing between, Western investors.

Business schools have a role to play here, and several have opened shop. One of the earliest was the Hungarian Management Institute which opened in Budapest in November 1988. The following year the International Management Centre also opened its doors in Budapest. Courses range from, 'Business English Communication' to a 'Young Manager Program' for the privileged few lucky enough to be sponsored by their companies or to receive scholarships. A stream of small, one-man consultancies are also being set up, often by expatriates who are familiar with the language and have a number of reliable contacts already established. There is a market for anyone with information, given the unfamiliarity of the terrain for both Western businessmen and Eastern enterprises and governments.

MANUFACTURING

As has been discussed in the earlier chapters, the Comecon countries indulged in substantial and often unsuitable industrialisation in the post-war years. As Comecon disintegrated, central planning started to dissolve and factories were suddenly faced with a need to achieve profitability. The whole scene had shifted. As Henryk Mędlewski of Polimex, a Polish chemicals enterprise, said, 'We have to change the profile of production in many factories. These new rules force our factories to change but ... it is not so easy to change from one day to another.' Bob Boland, chairman of Costain Engineering, which has been involved in a joint venture with Polimex for the last fifteen years, adds, 'In the short term it creates a lot of uncertainty while people adjust to the new system. Initially we have to be very realistic and say there are difficulties.' Mędlewski also admitted that in general, '[Polish] equipment is not compatible to world level.' On the other hand, he claims that some of the factories are 'quite well equipped with the essential machinery and equipment, but they have to change the organisation, economic system and salary system.'

The difficulties are extensive. Firstly, equipment is antiquated. As one of relatively few British industrial managers in Budapest, John Anthony of APV Baker is constantly being invited to come and look around factories with a view to recommending investment. 'If you look at most of the factories,' he says, 'the people are trying to work with equipment which is twenty or thirty years old. So instead of one man and a piece of decent machinery, you've got ten men hauling pieces of metal around, and using practices which [in the West] have been discontinued a long time ago.' Anthony estimates they must either reduce their staff by a factor of five or increase their productivity by the same amount in order to become profitable.

APV Baker, manufacturers of food-processing machinery, are trying one possible solution. Since wages, electricity and rents are cheaper than in the West, APV has opened a small factory 20km south-east of Budapest. Finding factory space was no problem, though offices were another matter. The machinery used in the factory is ten years old and came from APV's former Crawley factory where overheads of around £30 per hour meant it was no longer viable. The company simply shipped the machinery out to Budapest and reassembled it. APV now employs a dozen or so local people making pipe joints and Anthony is the only British manager. He expects the factory to become profitable within two years. APV Baker have thus made a minimal investment to ensure market presence and gain experience, while surveying the scene and waiting for other opportunities or for the economic climate to improve.

There is considerable bureaucracy involved in setting up and doing business in Eastern Europe. One estimate suggests that as many as 50,000 decrees govern economic life in Hungary. John Anthony provides an example of what happens if a crucial foreign-supplied part in his factory breaks. He must first get a quotation from the supplying company. APV has no licence for foreign trade, so he cannot order directly but must go to Complex, the state trading company responsible for the food business. Since it is very hard to get through on the telephone, this may involve a personal visit. He orders the part and pays for it. After about four weeks (if he keeps up the pressure on Complex to process his request) the order will arrive at the foreign supplying company. When the part eventually arrives in Budapest he has to summon the customs officer who must be present while he opens the package. All this time, unless the whole procedure can be circumvented in some way, the machinery in the factory stands still.

Through years of being repressed, people are now afraid to take decisions, and in the manufacturing industry this creates particular problems, primarily finding good managers. Harry Codd, chief executive of Ganz-Hunslet, a British-Hungarian locomotive manufacturer, explains, 'People were not known to be called on personally to take responsibility for the discharge of their duties or the quality of their work... None of them accepted responsibility for anything so they somehow became a sort of collective, and you couldn't really get hold of an individual.'

Existing factories are also heavily over-staffed. Anthony continues, 'Anybody buying into an existing manufacturing facility here may get some very cheap assets, but they would get a massively over-manned factory, working practices which should have been dispensed with forty or fifty years ago, managers who've never really been cost or profit accountable.' This has often led to mass redundancies when Western companies take over Eastern enterprises. One of the reasons Mrs Piasecka-Johnson's purchase of the Gdańsk shipyards fell through was because the level of redundancies was too high for the trade unions to stomach. Ryan International opened a small plant at Katowice in southern Poland with thirty-two workers, instead of the 250 which the Polish partners considered necessary. When Harry Codd took over at Ganz-Hunslet in Budapest, he was faced with reducing the numbers at the factory by half, from 1400 to 700. Even then he feared more would have to go.

Another problem that affects the cost of manufacturing in Eastern Europe is the heavy dependence on Soviet oil. The decision to convert all exports from roubles into hard currency from January 1991 hit hard at Eastern Europe's dollar-starved and energy-intensive heavy industry. Moreover, Soviet shortfalls after the ethnic turmoil in Azerbaijan in early 1990, and strikes in West Siberia, led to cutbacks and unreliable deliveries later in the year. The crisis in the Gulf and the rise in the price of oil did nothing to help. In July 1990, just before Iraq invaded Kuwait, Moscow cut oil supplies to Czechoslovakia by 30%. Prices rose, and rationing was introduced. Hungary, too, complained of falling supplies, and tried to impose a 65% price rise on petrol in October 1990, which provoked a major crisis for the government. Western investors should be aware of the possibility of Soviet oil being cut at irregular intervals.

There are, however, positive aspects to Eastern European manufacturing. Firstly, there is a large new market of potential consumers for the goods. Secondly, the workforce is skilled and educated, though not in new technologies and methods. The governments are keen to attract foreign investment, and all offer substantial tax benefits. Finally, salaries, rents and electricity costs are still lower than in the West.

Car manufacturers, for instance, have been moving in en masse[5]. Polski Fiat set up in Poland as long ago as 1921, and in 1965 started to produce Fiat 125s at the Warsaw FSO plant with an annual capacity of 70,000 cars. In 1970 Fiat progressed to making 150,000 126s each year at Bielsko Biała in Silesia. In September 1987 Fiat and FSM reached an agreement on producing a new car, the Micro, to be launched in 1991. Meanwhile FSO hoped to produce Fiat Tipos, though negotiations were protracted.

General Motors, Suzuki and Ford have invested in Hungary. The country previously produced no passenger cars, making it a huge importer. In Hungary, 68,000 cars were imported in 1989, but demand is still voracious. The waiting list of would-be buyers at the state-owned car importer, Merkur, stood at 260,000 in July 1990, in spite of a substantial increase in imports. General Motors formed a joint venture with Raba, a Hungarian group, to build engines and assemble passenger cars. Suzuki too began construction of an assembly plant in September 1990, to produce cars from 1992. Ford is to invest in a new plant producing ignition coils and fuel pumps. Ikarus, the main bus manufacturer in Hungary, used to export 90% of its output, but since dollar accounting began to replace roubles, it has experienced serious problems and tenders were invited from Western businesses in October 1990.

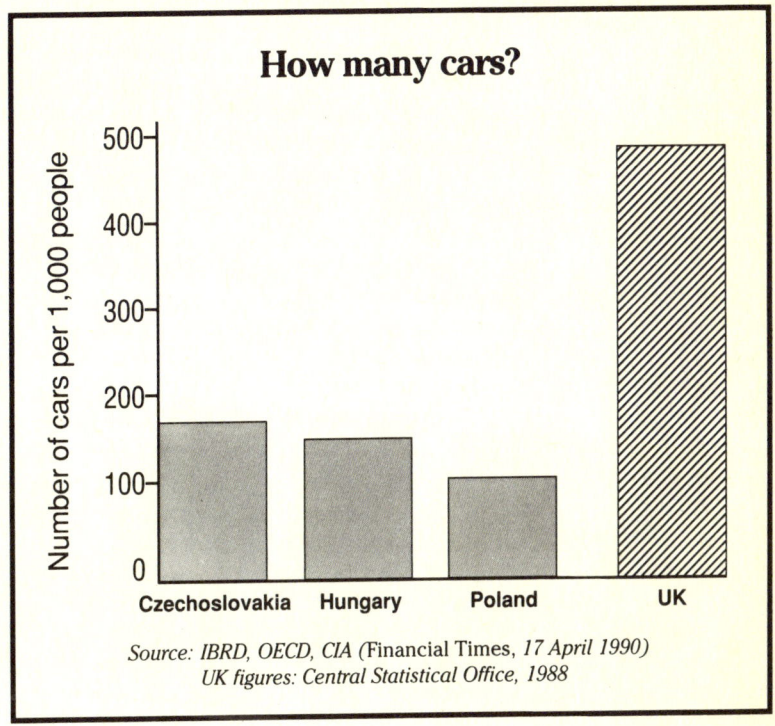

How many cars?

Number of cars per 1,000 people

Czechoslovakia   Hungary   Poland   UK

Source: IBRD, OECD, CIA (Financial Times, 17 April 1990)
UK figures: Central Statistical Office, 1988

With only 173 passenger cars per 1,000 population in Czechoslovakia, and 50% of cars on the road at least ten years old, the internal market has plenty of scope for expansion. Only 8,000 cars were sold per million inhabitants in 1989, though waiting lists were extensive. However, Škoda is Czechoslovakia's largest enterprise, and Eastern Europe's biggest car manufacturer. Road vehicles were the top import in 1989 from Czechoslovakia to the UK with a value totalling over £24 million.

In 1990 Škoda negotiated with different companies, including Fiat, Nissan, BMW, General Motors, Daimler-Benz and Renault, until after months of negotiations Volkswagen emerged as the winners. Škoda's basic initial conditions were typical of many Eastern European companies faced with joint-venture options or takeovers by Western companies. They hoped to maintain their identity and brand name, and to retain as many as possible of their staff whilst at the same time receiving investment to catch up with Western technology and production.

Smaller companies also attracted foreign interest. In 1990 Renault, Citroen, the South Korean company, KIA, and a part-British consortium competed to build a light commercial vehicle factory in Czechoslovakia. By May 1990, Toyota too was examining the possibilities of investment in the area. General Motors intended to start producing gearboxes in Czechoslovakia, and commenced negotiations with BAZ over the assembly of light commercial vehicles. Continental AG of West Germany signed a co-operation agreement with Czechoslovakia's largest tyre company, the state-owned Barum Group. It decided to invest in the Czechoslovak company in return for access to the new market. Barum Group is typical of this kind of large state enterprise: it has three major plants which employ 10,000 workers and produce together nearly 6 million tyres for cars and trucks. Annual sales for 1989 were about $441 million, unfortunately in non-convertible currency. It supplied the domestic market (i.e. Škoda) and other East European clients.

John Anthony of APV Baker summed up the attractions for manufacturers, 'There's a window of opportunity which is open here and will be for the next couple of years. I believe that the businesses that are not here establishing a good profile now, by the time the market is attractive enough for them to come here it will no longer be sufficiently open.' Other businessmen think the current window will stay open for five to seven years, and will then present more expensive, but nevertheless good opportunities for another decade after that.

Once again, the problem is how to operate profitably in Eastern Europe given the lack of hard currency. One potential solution is to form a joint venture with a manufacturer which could, perhaps with an injection of Western technology, export its products to convertible-currency markets. Export sales could provide a hard-currency cash flow which does not even enter the Eastern European country, and hence is not subject to the sometimes harsh rules on profit repatriation. Local currency costs would be covered by domestic sales of the product.

This is easier said than done, given the current low quality of almost all production in the area, lack of attractive or even secure packaging, unreliable transportation and communication and the often protected markets of Western countries. Nevertheless, it can be achieved, although at a considerable cost in both management time and money.

MEDICINE, PHARMACEUTICALS AND SCIENCE

Eastern European science is labouring under severe disadvantages. Previous academic progress relied at least partially on Communist party allegiance; contacts with Western scientists were severely limited by restrictions on travel, and are still restricted by lack of hard currency. Subscriptions to international journals such as *The Lancet* or *Nature* are out of the range of many Eastern pockets for both individuals and institutions. Status fell as scientists and manual workers earned similar salaries. More recently, university budgets came under threat with increasing financial constraints. Nevertheless, Eastern European scientists, Hungarians in particular, have a formidable reputation. From eight Nobel prizes to Rubik's cube, Hungarian scientists have much to offer the West. The Hungarian government spent a substantial 2.5% of gross national product on research.

Examples of academic scientists producing money-spinning inventions are not hard to find. One of the greatest success stories came from Czechoslovakia, where Otto Wichterle invented the soft contact lens in his own home in the 1960s. In Hungary, Béla Polyak at Vepex, a company owned by the Academy of Sciences, developed a new champagne fermentation technique which was taken over by a West German company. George Ferenczi patented a deep-level spectrometer, and in January 1990 he and his colleagues left their academic posts to form Semilab with capital from a West German company. Foment Ltd, a small British company formed by a Hungarian exile in Britain, took up an invention to control sulphur dioxide emissions. Frustrated by underfunding, however, many scientists, perhaps as many as 15% from Hungary, have emigrated, attracted by jobs and promises of research funding. The government, aware of this worrying brain drain, allocated extra funds in its 1991 budget to improve salaries for researchers.

Hungary has a well-established pharmaceutical industry which has for many years been supplying low-cost, high-quality antibiotics to the West. The leading companies, Gedeon Richter, Chinoin, Biogal and Reanal, were founded just after the war. Gedeon Richter, for instance, has a work-force of 6,000. The largest customer has traditionally been the Soviet Union, though exports to the West increased from 24.4% in 1987 to 34.7% in 1989[6]. The enterprise was among the first to be privatised in 1991, after valuation by accountants Coopers & Lybrand Deloitte.

Chinoin, with 4,500 workers, also plans to privatise. It recently discovered a new treatment for Parkinson's disease, Eldepryl, the first East European drug to be registered in the US, which is expected to bring in profits well in excess of $5 million annually. On a smaller scale, Cambridge Life Sciences entered into a joint venture with Vepex and two state banks to form Biotechnology International, initially to research into parasitic worms in humans and animals, and into an advanced method of extracting and purifying gamma linolenic acid, used in treating pre-menstrual tension, eczema and rheumatoid arthritis.

In total, the Hungarian pharmaceutical industry in 1990 represented 2% of Hungary's gross domestic product, and was a substantial foreign currency earner. What it needs, in common with other industries, is capital investment from the West. It also needs experience in trading directly with its customers, without the medium of Medimpex, the central trading corporation, which dealt with distribution, marketing and sales for the entire industry.

In general, as the *Financial Times* of 6 June 1990 concluded, 'Hungarian biotechnology, combined with Western funding, marketing and technical experience, could produce a valuable and profitable tonic.'

The chemical industry is another area of interest to the West, especially in Poland. A United Nations Industrial Development Organisation (UNIDO) programme was drawn up to increase petroleum-processing capacity by extending, modernising and adapting plants as necessary. New refineries were planned, for instance at Oswięcim, also known as Auschwitz. The manager of the chemical plant there blithely pointed out the efficiency of the local railway links, built by the Germans during the war. Now Germany, the United States, Britain and France are all interested in helping to restructure a chemical industry in Central Europe.

While Eastern Europe is looking to export to the West, the West is looking to export to the East. East European healthcare lags behind the rest of Europe, and not only in environmentally caused diseases. Standardised mortality rates, according to the World Health Organisation, are up to 40% higher in Eastern European countries than in Western, and much of the difference is accounted for by deaths from ischaemic heart disease and strokes (*British Medical Journal*, 11 August 1990). Stodgy diet, smoking, drinking and lack of exercise contribute to this tally. The average Czech eats 198 eggs and 46 kilos of meat *more* per year than the equivalent Briton. Only 12% of Hungarian women, as opposed to 60% of British women, have ever tried to diet (*The Independent*, 17 June

1990). These factors have led to a progressive fall in life expectancy, and Czechoslovakia and Hungary, once among the highest in Europe are now among the lowest, with Poland even lower.

Health education is lacking, but so are basic medical resources, especially in Poland. There is a lack of intravenous fluid and surgical gloves, to say nothing of drugs. Poland, for instance, makes only 15–20% of the needles and syringes it needs[7]. According to a report produced by the Association of British Health Care Industries and summarised in the *Health Care Journal*, October 1990, 'The East European healthcare market is ripe for a Western export drive.' It recommended an emphasis on cardiovascular products and drugs for stomach ailments. Of less interest were basic or routine pieces of equipment, which could be imported more cheaply from Third World countries. Companies are beginning to pay attention, and Glaxo, for instance, has formed a subsidiary to explore the market.

TOURISM

Tourism is one area which is already seeing a major boom, especially in Czechoslovakia and Hungary. Lake Balaton in Hungary has long been popular with Austrian and German tourists, while Czechoslovakia has a plethora of wonderful attractions; the alpine Tatra, the castles of Bohemia and the vineyards of Slovakia and Moravia. Budapest, with its reputation as a thriving cultural centre, with restaurants and gypsy dancing, and Prague, with its beautiful buildings ranging through the centuries from medieval to baroque to art nouveau, have never lacked for admirers. Positive media coverage has made Eastern Europe flavour of the decade, and the number of visitors has been soaring way above what can be comfortably handled by existing facilities. Hungary, for instance, saw nearly 25 million tourists in 1989, a rise of 39%, while figures for the first half of 1990 showed an unprecedented rise of 80%[8] over the previous year. Czechoslovakia saw an even steeper increase, with over 17 million visitors in just the first half of 1990. The number of Eastern Bloc visitors rose 50% over the same period the previous year, while the number of Western visitors rose 500%. Polish and Austrian travellers predominated.

Hard-currency earnings from tourism increased correspondingly, but potential was still far below capacity. While

Czechoslovakia earned only $150 million in 1989, Austria earned $9 billion. Hungary expected hard-currency spending for 1990 to reach only $800 million, although this was double that of the previous year.

Hungarians, Czechs and Poles have also been able to travel freely for the first time since the war, and this has caused a hard-currency deficit, especially for Hungary. In 1989 Hungarian tourism earned $740 million, but millions of Hungarians rushing over the border, mainly to Austria, managed to spend $1.07 billion. The number of Czechs travelling abroad has increased from 853,000 in the first quarter of 1989 to 2,713,000 for the same period a year later. Unlike the Western tourists in Eastern Europe, the Czechs and Poles do not tend to spend hard currency freely, and residents of favoured towns such as Berlin and Venice have begun to complain.

Travel agencies in both directions have been swamped by demand, and in June 1990 the London branch of Cedok, the Czech state tourist agency, was so overwhelmed that it closed its doors until October, unable to handle private tourists. Businessmen too have found a shortage of hotel space, and while hotels such as the Marriott in Warsaw or the Forum in Budapest are well up to international standards, others, especially in Prague, are not. Hotel construction was neglected over the last twenty years, and those that were built were often shoddily constructed and highly priced with outrageously poor service. Private rental is now supplementing official hotel space, while new hotels are being constructed apace, especially in the Czech capital. Competition to buy hotels is fierce among Western investors. The manager of the Praha Hotel, the ex-private Communist party hotel, apologised for offering a business card lacking the fax number. 'I'm waiting to print new ones,' he said, 'but I don't know whether to print Praha-Marriott, or Praha-Meridien, or whatever.'

More sophisticated development of tourism has yet to make its impact in Czechoslovakia or Poland. Czechoslovakia, for instance, has ski areas which are underdeveloped, and although there are pleasant facilities in the High Tatra, these are only adequate to cope with previous, mainly internal demand. Fishing and climbing facilities could be extended. The spa towns, such as Karlovy Vary and Marianské Lázně, already have a reputation outside Czechoslovakia, although facilities could do with refurbishing. A casino was opened in Karlovy Vary in 1987 as a joint venture between Casino Austria and Balnex, and proved so successful that seven further casinos are planned in Prague hotels. Other foreign ventures include a Swedish company which is looking to build a hotel complex with golf course.

Western hotel chains have their eye on the 'new' European capitals and need to establish a presence here. During a trade fair all rooms in Budapest, fairly well served in comparison to the other two capitals, are invariably taken. With Expo 95 looming on the horizon, hotel construction is likely to take a higher priority. It is estimated that 90 billion forints ($1.4 billion) will have to be spent on infrastructural projects in Hungary linked to the Expo alone. Meanwhile, the hotel developer hoping to move into the Czech market is advised to book his own room months in advance.

PROPERTY AND ARCHITECTURE

This is an area bristling with opportunity as companies looking for office space, retailers keen to show their goods on main streets, and hotels eager to lodge the new hordes of tourists, all jostle for space in what was one of the world's most restricted property markets. It is also an area fraught with legal difficulties. Some of the property was confiscated by the Nazis during the last war, and yet more was confiscated by the communists in the 1950s. The original owners are now turning up clutching their property deeds, and this situation needs to be sorted out before the market can relax. In Czechoslovakia, a six-month 'sorting-out' period for owners to present their claims was declared between November 1990 and April 1991. Meanwhile, legal restrictions still control large sectors. In Poland, in June 1990, it was still officially illegal to own more than one house. A major development of the business quarter in Budapest hoping to go ahead in July 1990, decided to await municipal elections in the autumn to be sure of the last stages of Hungary's political transformation.

The whole concept of an estate agent was, until recently, completely foreign. Anthony Spencer, an estate agent planning to set up in Prague, commented wearily, 'It's very difficult to find anything or do anything. Basically the people don't really know what capitalism is. They have an idea, they try and make it up as they go along. But to try and get a decision is very difficult.'

Since foreigners are prevented from buying property in Czechoslovakia, rental is often the only option. Here, too, Spencer encountered difficulties. 'We went in to see a gentleman who owned a building in the [Wenceslas] square and asked him how much he wanted to rent the building for ... Initially he didn't comprehend the word "rent", he didn't understand because no one has actually rented a building here for the last fifty years... There's no comprehension of what a rent or a yield – or anything – is here.' Spencer found people asking £60 per square foot in Prague, similar to London rents.

A CASE STUDY
British architect Jiřina Jackson stood up at a conference in Bratislava in March 1990 and invited Czechoslovak colleagues interested in co-operation with Western companies to get in contact. She was immediately inundated with requests. By the end of the week she had a stack of business cards five centimetres high from which to choose. A few weeks later she returned, this time accompanied by one of the directors of D.Y.Davies Associates, a large architectural firm, to investigate the possibilities of the new market. D.Y.Davies had already established associations with studios throughout Western Europe, and Czechoslovakia seemed like a natural extension.

A series of meetings ensued. It was hard to know to whom to speak first. Under the old system, all projects came from the state, and nearly all were carried out by State Institutes. These Institutes made welcoming though discreet noises, preparing their safety nets for eventual privatisation. Other state architects were splitting off and forming independent studios. All clamoured for attention. One representative of an agricultural co-operative with 600 staff in tiny units dispersed throughout Czechoslovakia was particularly persistent. 'I had people queuing up in the hotel foyer to come and see me,' said Tim Forsyth, one of D.Y.Davies' directors. 'There were people door-stepping us in the coffee bar.' Eventually he narrowed his choice down to two government departments, the Prague Design Institute (PPU) and the State Institute for the Reconstruction of Historic Towns and Monuments (SURPMO). The eventual aim seemed to be some form of joint venture.

The PPU is one of the largest state enterprises dealing in the construction of public buildings in Czechoslovakia. It employed 800 staff, 120 of whom were architects. The rest were construction and structural engineers, utilities managers and administrators. Its past projects ranged from housing estates to hotels and swimming pools. The PPU is responsible for some fairly successful estates around Prague's suburbs, such as the twenty-year-old Dablice, but its most recent complex is the notorious Jižni Město, containing 10,500 flats around a shabby shopping centre. The PPU's showpiece is the Praha Hotel, opened in 1981. Constructed as the private hotel of the Communist party it is gloriously decadent, with vast monumental staircases, winter garden and superb swimming pool. The PPU directors speak proudly of the hotel's 205,000m^3 volume and 73,000m^2 area. Possible investors would rather hear about budget targets and occupancy rates.

At SURPMO, the meetings took place under a painted Renaissance ceiling. Responsible primarily for restoration of historic buildings, this Institute has an international reputation. The majority of buildings in Staroměstské Náměsti, the Old Town Square, or at Hradčany, the castle area, bear witness to the quality of SURPMO's work. It also carries out other projects, such as urban design studies, mainly in Yugoslavia or the Middle East. It too employed 800 staff. On DYD's possible contribution here, Forsyth noted, 'We've got a lot of experience in turning old and historic buildings to new uses so that they can generate the income that is necessary to keep them in order.'

The negotiations with the companies were convoluted and there were extra twists caused by working in an unknown area. Would the differences in culture, language and working methods prove too great? As for the profit motive: 'Now that's something they haven't got much experience of in Czechoslovakia,' commented Forsyth. Jiřina Jackson summarised some other problems, 'There is a general lack of appreciation of the concept of building contracts ... existing safety regulations and standards are not in line with those adopted in the West. Information and knowledge of Western building products is also very limited.' DYD's lawyer, David Walker, joined the talks and found he had to start from scratch. How could you negotiate the number of seats on the board when the other party did not understand the concept of a board? Could DYD repatriate any profits? Did the Czech directors even have the right to negotiate the ownership of their enterprise? Did DYD have the right to make people redundant, given the huge numbers of staff at each Institute?

Jiřina Jackson and Tim Forsyth went to consult Pavel Weishaupt, the deputy minister of planning, architecture and construction, sitting in an office overflowing with paperwork, and reached by a classic paternoster lift. A Havel look-alike, chain-smoking and witty, Weishaupt gave DYD his blessing.

Continually interrupted by architects handing in forms to apply for the new certificate of professional competence which he had just created, Weishaupt explained that his role was to create the conditions for Czechoslovakia to rejoin the rest of Europe. He had just come from meetings with another British company, Gleeds, with whom he was trying to create the profession of Chartered Quantity Surveyor, which in Eastern Europe has been hitherto unknown. He was also talking to the Royal Institute of British Architects about trying to draw up a professional code of conduct for Czech architects.

Armed with the assurance that the Czech government approved of the negotiations, Forsyth continued his talks. Both Czech enterprises hoped for capital investment and staff training. The PPU initially seemed willing to accept almost any terms, but as negotiations reached a climax, it brought in an advisor from the Czech Chamber of Commerce. Finally the two parties agreed to form an association for specific projects, rather than an all-embracing joint venture.

SURPMO, meanwhile, proved harder to pin down. When Forsyth went to his meeting with Petr Plachy, deputy director of SURPMO, Plachy was not there. He had apparently gone to London to meet Forsyth. Other misunderstandings dogged the negotiations, but eventually a deal was signed under similar conditions to the PPU agreement – co-operation on specific projects. In each case the design stages of the project would probably be carried out in London with a team of British and Czech architects. The production drawing stages would then transfer back to Prague.

Forsyth professed himself well satisfied with his efforts. 'There's certainly a will and I think an understanding by the architects here that they've got a new opportunity, a new start.' Meanwhile Jiřina Jackson organised a property conference in Prague. One of the keynote speeches was entitled, 'Function of the Estate Agent'!

RETAIL

Eastern Europe has 130 million potential consumers, not including another 280 million in the Soviet Union. For years these people were restricted in what they could buy, afflicted by shortages and poor quality goods. Then suddenly public demand for Western goods had a chance of being satisfied. Through the years, as few goods were available, people hoarded their money, especially hard currency. Now this 'currency overhang', whose existence is sometimes disputed, and whose size is unknown, is being used to buy goods, from satellite dishes to cars and cosmetics. In Czechoslovakia, for instance, savings deposits are thought to account for 57% of personal incomes (see graph on page 69). The comparative shortage of retail outlets to deal with the new demand and the relaxation of legislative controls as the governments of Czechoslovakia, Hungary and Poland facilitate the move to a market economy make this area interesting for Western business.

Retailing – like everything else – used to be centrally controlled to a greater or lesser extent[9]. In Czechoslovakia 99% of retail outlets were either directly state controlled or state co-operatives. In 1988 the government relaxed its terms very slightly to allow citizens to run small shops and restaurants leased from the state. Only family members were to be employed and profits were strictly controlled. As Jaromir Zak, the then finance minister, said in an interview with the *Financial Times*, October 1987, 'The state will make sure no-one gets rich on this.'

It was not until early 1990 that the first Czechoslovak businesses, mainly small shops, services and workshops, escaped from the all-embracing state mantle. A small proportion of state shops under the old system were Tuzex hard-currency shops. The Tuzex stores, of which there were only about 100, sold everything from cars to razors, foodstuffs to electrical goods. Helena Felix, of Aquascutum, who worked with Tuzex for fifteen years, explained the phenomenon. 'Tuzex was started to give people the chance to spend their money in their own country. Twenty-five years ago if somebody had $10 they said to a friend who happened to be going to Vienna on a business trip, "Buy me a black shirt," and then if it didn't fit he couldn't change it... While Tuzex is anachronistic, people who could get hard currency could buy the goods.' The shops ran their own currency, 'Tuzex crowns', vouchers which could only be bought for hard currency, and which were at one time worth about three ordinary crowns. They could be kept in special Tuzex bank accounts, but were abolished as of January 1991. 'Of course it's an anachronism,' said Helena Felix. 'But you can't change overnight everything that has been going on for forty-one years.' Tuzex was a shop for the elite – the *nomenklatura*, the diplomats – or once a year for the ordinary citizen. Meanwhile the ordinary citizen supplemented purchases by having recourse to the black market. It is estimated that this accounted for as much as 10% of personal income.

Aware that a lot of the political unrest stemmed from economic dissatisfaction, the government relaxed control of the major department stores in 1989, permitting them to retain some hard currency from their allocation for buying Western goods. In 1990 the black market was semi-legalised in the form of street markets, and private retail outlets are now being established. Retail trade turnover increased in the first four months of 1990 by 7.1%, half of which probably came from tourism. (See Chapter 5 for information about privatisation.)

Hungary is much further advanced towards a free retail market. Paul Southworth, managing director of Avon Cosmetics, which has been selling in Hungary since early 1990, commented, 'I think basically Hungary is more developed in terms of their approach to Western culture and Western business than the other Eastern countries at the moment. And because of that this is obviously the place to be early, so that we can understand the Eastern economics and dynamics, and at the same time use Hungary long-term as a springboard for all our future Eastern Bloc activities.' He did, however, recommend a cautious approach, 'It's very important that you establish the right relationships, both at the government level and with the trading ministers. Understanding the market-place itself, what is the retail environment, what are the stores selling, what kind of price structure exists, and so on.'

Hungarian shops are well stocked and goods attractively displayed. Western companies such as Benetton and McDonalds are in evidence, but only in Budapest. Foreign currency purchases increased in 1989 by a huge 84.2%. Price controls have now been freed on most goods. Some 40% of outlets are run by private traders, although these are usually the smaller stores.

In the early 1980s 'economic working associations' (GMK's) were legalised, allowing small businesses to employ up to thirty-five people. This boosted the retail trade in particular and by 1988 there were 25,600 private traders. In 1988 there were still 38,000 state and co-operative stores, but over 4,000 of these had some kind of profit deal with the managers. These, however, worked under considerable disadvantages. They had to accept whatever goods were offered by the manufacturers, even if quality and fashion were not interesting. They had to allocate a fixed area of floorspace to each department, regardless of requirements and they had to take all goods at the state-fixed price, with no room for manoeuvre or negotiation.

In 1990 inflation began to affect retail sales. Figures for the first half of 1990 showed a drop of 10.3% in real terms. Individual earnings rose by 22.2%, but the rise was eaten up by inflation. Savings, however, increased.

Of the three countries examined here, Poland's retail trade was in the worst situation. Until the recent changes most outlets were state-owned. Non-food shops were owned and run by the WPHW (Wojewódzkie Przedsiębiorstwa Handlu Wewnętrznego, the Provincial Organisation for Internal Trade), or in Warsaw, the SPHW. Department stores and supermarkets also existed, but were fairly thin on the ground. State subsidies on many consumer goods accounted for 31% of state spending in 1989, and affected nearly 42% of the budget of each household. These were slashed in early 1990 as part of the government's stringent austerity plans, and prices have consequently risen sharply.

In 1988 13% of shops were privately owned, an increase of around 100% over the previous decade. Now a typical sight on the streets of Warsaw is a large lorry with its back open selling direct to the public. No overheads, no taxes, no statistics.

The equivalent of the Czech Tuzex hard-currency shops was the Pewex chain of 800 outlets, selling a narrower range of luxury goods and imported items than Tuzex. Pewex is to be privatised in the near future. Several Western stores, such as Benetton and Puma, also sold in hard currency, but gradually as the zloty achieved convertibility all these, Pewex included, started to mark up, first in zloties and dollars, then simply in zloties.

In a survey carried out for the European Commission, Price Waterhouse's David Jeary summarised the key characteristics of Eastern European retailing: 'Low density of outlets. Small crowded shops. Poorly paid shop staff. Three-queue system (queue for the goods, queue to pay for the goods, queue to pick up the goods). Narrow product ranges. Limited import rights. Low capital investment. Lack of competition.' There is obviously room for improvement.

There is equally obviously a demand for goods, especially quality goods. When border controls were briefly lifted in late 1989, the Hungarians streamed across the border to Austria and spent millions of dollars before a $50 annual maximum allowance for foreign travel was slapped on. Avon Cosmetics, which went in to Hungary with the company's standard direct selling method, exceeded its first three-month quota of goods in the initial six weeks of operations. No doubt encouraged by this success, other cosmetics groups such as the Swedish Oriflame International set up subsidiaries.

Poles queued for hours in the first Benetton in Warsaw to buy brightly coloured jumpers, and spend their precious dollars. A survey by Landor Associates carried out in July 1990 showed that the East was well acquainted with Western and Japanese brand names, especially those associated with high quality goods. Helena Felix of Aquascutum commented, 'The Czechs are very clever people. They won't buy the world's rubbish. They're very sophisticated, have got very good taste, and they won't be the world's dumping ground.' However, according to the survey, Hungarians were the most worldly, recognising an average 250 out of 400 brand names, while the Poles knew 175. In Poland, for instance, the top ten were Sony, Volvo, Mercedes-Benz, Adidas, Toyota, Ford, BMW, Philips, Porsche and Honda. The only British names to appear on the Hungarian top ten were Rolls-Royce and Jaguar, which made it to number six and seven respectively. According to Sarah Greenwood of Landor, interviewed in *The European*, 3 August 1990, 'Car brands do well in the survey because cars represent choice, luxury and freedom.' Cars are another sector where, for years, demand has exceeded supply.

In the opposite direction, there are some retail goods of interest for export. Optics, glassware, chinaware, hardware, some foodstuffs and toys have been successful in the past. It is estimated that foreign purchases accounted for 3% of Czech retail sales in 1989. Austrians and Germans have earned criticism by nipping across the border and filling up with anything from salami to crystal glass at the cheaper Czech and Hungarian prices.

In general, prospects in retail seem promising in Poland unless inflation and recession destroy the population's buying capacity. They will probably be promising in Czechoslovakia once the government has worked out how to proceed in opening up the economy. Hungary meanwhile already looks like a very interesting market and one that is attracting much attention from the West.

CHAPTER 5

THE MECHANICS OF BUSINESS

This chapter takes a closer look at some of the current business issues in Eastern Europe. In particular it investigates joint ventures, privatisation, import/export and counter-trade.

The phrase 'joint venture' has become a catchword, attractive to the East and acceptable to the West, and the formula is proving to be one of the most popular vehicles of investment for Eastern Europe. Although foreign investors can establish a new, completely foreign-owned company, joint ventures often seem to be a relatively safe option. They can be formed by the foreign company acquiring shares in existing companies, by creating a new joint venture from scratch with local partners, or simply by co-operating with an existing company. This section looks at the legal background in each country. It then provides some information about choosing a partner and setting up the joint venture, and also draws the businessman's attention to a few of the problems to which joint ventures are subject.

All three countries are embarking on massive privatisation programmes designed to attract foreign investment and de-monopolise their economy. We look at the different approaches adopted and their chances of success.

Import and export organisations are then discussed, followed by an analysis of counter-trade, often considered a necessary evil in trading with Eastern Europe.

JOINT VENTURES

No sector is excluded; joint ventures have been created in everything from service industries to heavy industry. Western companies gain a local partner familiar with the language and business customs of the area, able to locate or possibly already in possession of offices or factory space, with local contacts and workforce, and perhaps even with a ready-made market for the eventual products. The East European partner hopes to gain management training, Western technology and expertise, access to new markets and, of course, an injection of valuable foreign currency.

While foreigners can now legally own and operate their own companies in these countries, there are many advantages, especially in the form of tax concessions and risk minimisation, in creating a joint venture. Local governments are particularly keen to encourage this form of co-operation and there is often a good deal of pressure on the Western European partner to choose this method. Dr Yochanan Altman of Cranfield Management School sums up the reasoning behind this: 'For the economies of Eastern Europe, the only hope is through joint ventures.'

LEGAL BACKGROUND

Czechoslovakia

The first steps towards legalising joint ventures were taken by the Czechoslovak government in 1985. At that time joint companies were permitted to operate only in the industrial production sector. This showed a clear desire to channel co-operation towards areas where technological progress was involved and where Czechoslovak enterprises could be expected to benefit most from Western innovation. The following year, in an effort to share information and rationalise the internal market, Comecon members signed an agreement regulating joint ventures between enterprises belonging to the Comecon area.

In 1987 Czechoslovakia relaxed the rules on joint ventures slightly, to attract firms involved in the development of tourism. This area, along with computer technology, electronics, and precision machine tools was considered a priority sector by the Czechoslovak government. During 1988 and 1989 further changes were introduced into Czechoslovak joint-venture legislation, but the lack of clarity, and uncertainty about investment and profit repatriation guarantees meant that foreign investors reacted very cautiously. Investors had to rely on exceptional provisions granted by the authorities for their particular case, rather than on an easily workable, non-subjective legal framework.

The first joint ventures with Western partners were set up at the end of 1987, and served as a small scale experiment for the state to consider their value as a way of doing business. By mid 1988 the structure had been shown to work, though it was not easy to set up. By the time the Communist government fell there were only about fifty joint ventures. Eleven were in the field of tourism or medical care at spa resorts and only twelve were in industrial production. In terms of countries, Austria was the largest partner with thirteen ventures.

The would-be joint venturer had to follow a cumbersome and confused procedure. Stephen Holby, export finance manager of Barclays Bank, described his experience in April 1990. The company involved wished to set up a joint venture production plant. 'As the Czechoslovak partner was a producer co-operative, it had to go first to the Union of Producer Co-operatives, and then to its ministry. It then had either to involve a Foreign Trade Organisation or obtain foreign trade rights by application to the State Bank and the Ministry for Foreign Trade before we could involve the Czechoslovak Commercial Bank in financing the importation of the necessary equipment.' Holby continued, 'Clearly this lengthy bureaucratic process had to be simplified and ... barriers started to fall as we approached them.' Even as he was speaking, new laws were being passed.

The 1988 Act on Enterprise with Foreign Property Participation was radically modified in May 1990 to permit far greater freedom for both foreign and Czechoslovak parties[1]. Firstly, Czechoslovak individuals were given equal legal status with Czechoslovak corporate bodies; previously they were not allowed to participate at all. Foreign parties were given a greater choice of partner – they could, for instance, buy into an existing joint-venture corporation. In fact, they no longer really needed to find a Czechoslovak partner at all. Originally only Czechoslovak majority interests were permitted, then in 1988 foreign parties were allowed a majority holding. Finally, under the new amendments all such restrictions were abolished. Minimum investment was 100,000 crowns ($4,200) and the old system, trotting from ministry to ministry, under which Holby suffered, was simplified.

Business partners could now choose any national law they wished to govern the contract. In other words, they were no longer restricted to the Czechoslovak legal system. They could do business in almost all sectors, national defence and security excepted. The foreign exchange legislation, however, was tightened up. Instead of being able to dispose of their foreign exchange balances as they wished, joint ventures were now obliged to offer to sell 30% of their foreign exchange earnings to the appropriate Czechoslovak bank. They also needed authorisation from the State Bank to open a hard-currency account with a foreign bank.

In general, the legislation has been welcomed by the business community. By October 1990, 500 joint ventures had been set up, with a dozen or so new ones approved every day. Many of these, however, are for small companies, involving the minimum 100,000 crowns' ($4,200) capital investment. The most attractive sectors are trade, services, tourism and consulting[2].

Hungary

Hungary has traditionally been far more welcoming towards foreign economic participation, and therefore has greater experience in this field. Joint ventures have been permitted since 1972, but unfavourable economic and legal conditions meant that only ten were created in the first decade. They only really began to make an impact in the late 1980s when the rules were simplified and attractive incentives introduced.

The main pieces of legislation were the Act on Economic Associations (Company Act) and the Act on Foreign Investment in Hungary, 1988. These were passed with the declared intention of encouraging foreign investment directly in Hungarian enterprises, as well as in joint ventures, by laying down the basis of a market-orientated integration of enterprises. State-owned enterprises and co-operatives were put on an equal legal footing with private businesses, an obvious reform to Western eyes. Foreigners were now even permitted to own entire companies. Joint ventures were all to be registered with the Court of Registration, but if the foreign share exceeded 50% the case was referred up to the ministers of finance and of trade for joint permission, with an upper limit of ninety days' delay. For less than 50% foreign ownership official permission was no longer needed. Foreign companies were particularly encouraged to read that the new Act meant investments of foreigners in Hungary would enjoy 'full protection and security', and that in the case of nationalisation or expropriation they would be compensated 'without delay', and in the currency in which the original investment had taken place.

Once the legal obstacles had been removed, companies began to enter the market, and the number of joint ventures began to increase substantially. Between 1974 and 1988, only 228 joint ventures were founded in Hungary. By January 1989 there were 280 more joint ventures with a total foreign investment of $300 million. Austria and West Germany led the way, both in terms of the number of joint ventures, and of the foreign capital committed, but the Swiss, French and Italians also provided a significant presence. The most popular sectors were trade, tourism and the service industry, especially consultancy, though the largest single investments were in manufacturing. General Electric took just over 50% of Tungsram, a leading light-bulb manufacturer, for $150 million; General Motors put $100 million into buying 67% of a joint venture with Raba, the automotive engineering group.

Joint ventures can be carried out in any kind of business. Budapest's McDonalds for instance, is a 50:50 joint venture between McDonalds and the Hungarian agro-industrial complex, Babolna. Babolna supplied premises and furnishings, McDonald's the technical kitchen equipment and some hard currency. All profits are to be reinvested for the first five years.

By June 1990 there were an estimated 1,800 joint ventures, as opposed to only 280 a year earlier. Of these, 300 involved German capital, and 300 Austrian. The total foreign working capital by then was estimated at around $700 million, up from $150 million a year before. Only in one third of joint ventures did the foreign stake exceed 50%. Half were in manufacturing and half in trading activities, and while the Austrian and German companies predominated, businessmen from over forty countries had invested in Hungarian joint ventures. By September 1990 there were over 2,500 joint ventures with foreign participation.

Poland

The laws governing joint ventures in Poland have also been modified several times, always to enhance their attraction for foreign investors. Joint ventures first became legal in 1986, but the initial response was poor, mainly because the Polish partner was obliged to retain majority ownership, taxes were very high, and a proportion of the hard-currency revenue had to be sold back to the National Bank irrespective of the company's future plans. Coupled with Poland's rather uncertain political and economic status, this had discouraged the formation of joint ventures and it became obvious that if Poland wanted to promote this form of foreign investment, new legislation was urgently needed. The main Act on Economic Activity with the Participation of Foreign Parties (The Foreign Investment Law) was therefore passed in December 1988, but modified a year later. The expressed aim was 'to create stable conditions for further development of mutually advantageous capital co-operation between Polish and foreign parties, to guarantee to foreign parties the protection of their property, income and other rights.' Foreign investors could now be either companies or individuals. A Polish citizen living abroad was now considered to be the same as any other foreign investor, whereas under the old system 'Polonia' – people of Polish origin living abroad – had had a special status. Foreign investors could now establish a limited liability company and own 100% of the equity. They could establish a limited liability or joint-stock company with equity contributed by founders together with other

foreign or Polish parties. They could raise equity through public
subscription of shares. They could buy shares in existing companies, though if there were no foreign shareholders before purchase,
they were obliged to increase the equity of the company. Joint
ventures could be established with just about everyone – state
enterprises, the Treasury, research institutes, universities, co-operatives, companies and individuals. They could be established in
every field of activity, and there were no limits on the size of the
company. The only restriction was that 'the share of foreign parties
may not be lower than 20% of the company's subscribed equity'
and that the minimum contribution be over $50,000. Foreign
currency and zloty profit could be transferred freely.

The Act also established the Foreign Investment Agency to
help formulate state policy on foreign investment co-operation,
stimulate more foreign interest and supervise companies wishing
to set up. The agency was a small, modern organisation which
dealt with all aspects of foreign investment – from welcoming
foreign queries, to trying to pair would-be investors with suitable
partners, providing guidance through the maze of bureaucracy
and issuing the initial permits. The offices were designed to look
very different from the usual Polish government bureaux, with
stylish black tables and chairs on pine floors, and highly trained,
multi-lingual staff. The newness of the subject and the volume of
enquiries, however, meant that there were criticisms of the agency's work. 'You must take into account all the profound trans-
formations, the radical changes in this part of the world, and in
Poland specifically,' Zbigniew Piotrowski, president of the FIA,
defended the work of his agency. 'We are changing the laws. We
are changing administrative procedures, and also we are changing
organisations, institutions.' One of the problems was that when
the agency was originally established, foreign investment was not
such a high priority as it has now become. 'The agency was
established to be a one-stop agency,' said Piotrowski, but his staff
of fifty or so were soon cutting back on the 'total concept' of foreign
investment from promotion through selection and negotiation, to
government advice on future legislation. The sensible solution,
assuming foreign interest remains high, would be to concentrate
on the smooth processing of registration of new joint ventures, and
leave commercial companies to fill the gaps by, for instance,
providing negotiating counsel. An internal analysis carried out in
June 1990 showed that applications were dealt with in an average
of three weeks. Delays were generally caused by specific difficulties,
such as queries over valuation of the assets of state-owned com-

panies. In such cases, application could take a couple of months. Usually, however, delays were caused simply because one of the vital pieces of documentation was missing.

The Polish government is particularly keen to encourage joint-venture investment in certain sectors. These include any activity which brings in modern technology and management methods, which provides goods and services for exports, which improves the supply of modern and high quality products and services for the domestic market, and which protects the environment. Such proposals are likely to receive priority treatment.

The number of registered joint ventures has gradually increased. Between 1986 and 1988 there were only fifty-two, half that for the month of July 1990 alone. By September 1990 about 2,000 joint venture permits had been registered by the Foreign Investment Agency. These figures, however, indicate ventures registered but not necessarily operational, and most of these are only fairly small investments. Companies with the minimum capital investment ($50,000) prevail. Though the investments are small, the volume of registrations indicates much interest. German investors predominate (41%), followed by Swedes (9.5%) and Austrians (7%).

CHOOSING A PARTNER

No businessman needs to be told that choosing a partner whom he can trust is one of the most crucial stages in forming a successful joint venture. Since Eastern Europe is such unknown territory, with fast-changing legislation and unfamiliar languages, where personal contacts may be of essential importance, choice of partner requires perhaps even greater attention. As a newspaper advertisement for the Polish Economic Society states, in succinct English: 'Rightly chosen partner is half success.'

All three countries have by now set up several data banks listing enterprises according to type of business. The main one in Czechoslovakia is at the Chamber of Commerce, in Hungary, at the Investcenter, and in Poland, at the Office of Promotion of the Foreign Investment Agency, or at the Economic Data Bank of the Solidarity Economic Foundation. Some of these organisations charge a small fee for information, but most simply hand out thick volumes listing enterprises seeking foreign investment. Local newspapers in English are full of contact names of 'consultants' specialising in different sectors, and international consultancy firms have set up branches to offer advice, at a price, and many expatriates in Britain are setting up small consultancies.

Finding a joint-venture partner may be a matter of pure luck.

Jo Malins of the British firm Hunslet Holdings spent several months unsuccessfully looking for a Polish partner. One weekend he played tennis with a Hungarian friend who, when he heard of the search, pointed Malins in the direction of Ganz-Mavag, a state-owned locomotive enterprise about to be broken up and sold off. Similarly, a Swiss-Polish croissant shop in Warsaw came about when the partners met at a hotel in a tourist resort and had to share a table one evening. Most joint ventures, however, will be underpinned by a lot of hard work and finally by a risk-taking commitment. Given the unreliability of accounts under the old system and the uncertainty of future business, with old trading relationships completely transformed, personal judgement will usually have to take precedence over much of the systematic 'due diligence' material usual in the West. Do the assets appear sound? Does he trust his partners? Oliver Letwin, head of privatisation at N.M. Rothschilds & Sons summed up the difficulties of choice at a conference in London in May 1990: 'How do you decide where to joint venture and how quickly do you do so, and how willing are you to get your fingers burnt and how many fingers.'[3]

SETTING UP JOINT VENTURES

Czechoslovakia
Before registration the Czechoslovak partner must open a security deposit with a minimum investment from the venture of 100,000 crowns ($4,200). All applications for authorisation are to be addressed to the Federal Ministry of Finance, which should take a decision within sixty days, unless the activities are in the financial sector, in which case the Czechoslovak State Bank also needs to give permission. Foreign licences are issued by the Ministry of Foreign Trade. Advice is given from the Czechoslovak Chamber of Commerce.

Hungary
In order to set up a joint venture in Hungary the deed or articles of association must be signed by all participants and witnessed by a lawyer. This deed must include: the name and address of the company; the members, with their names and addresses; the range of activities of the company and the size of the company's assets. All joint ventures must notify the Court of Registration of the foundation of the association within thirty days of establishment, along with the necessary documentation. The foreign party's cash contribution must be paid 'in a freely convertible currency', but

in-kind contributions in the form of 'any negotiable asset with a real value, any intellectual property and any valuable right' are acceptable. Joint ventures need to register with the Ministry of Commerce if they wish to conduct foreign trade, and also require special permits for some activities, such as construction work.

Although the registration sounds fairly straightforward, in practice the current popularity of joint ventures and the relative inexperience of the staff handling the registration can cause some inconvenience. According to Laszlo Sugar, managing director of Chemo Iberica, a Spanish-Hungarian joint venture set up in 1990, even if the businessman (or preferably his lawyers) manages to get all the correct papers together and they are accepted without question, he still needs to set aside five or six hours to queue for the authorising stamp on his papers. Other businessmen describe how each registry court seems to have its own method of working, and in a totally arbitrary fashion the officials sometimes request additional documentation. Some have been turned away because of a typographical error in one of the forms. Until the businessman is registered, he will experience problems opening a bank account, organising his taxes or renting office space.

Poland
In Poland applications for the permit must be addressed to the Foreign Investment Agency, and must include a draft of the foundation act, documentary evidence as to the legal status and financial standing of prospective shareholders, and an economic and financial feasibility study of the company, which must include market and financial surveys and 'techno-organisational analysis'. Proof of the minimum $50,000 deposit must also be given.

PROBLEMS
Joint ventures are well recognised as being a difficult way to run a business. Just as any marriage between very different partners may have rocky patches, and may even founder, so joint ventures are fraught with difficulty, though are often rewarding.

One of the main problems is that the two partners have such different aspirations that they may eventually prove incompatible. Western companies are often hoping simply to gain access to a new market, while the Eastern counterpart is hoping for exactly the same thing in the opposite direction. While the Western investors' funds may be locked into a non-convertible currency, the Eastern partner is looking for hard currency through investment and increased exports.

There may be further disappointments in the level of commitment of the Western partner. The technology offered may sometimes be of mediocre quality. Several companies setting up, especially in Hungary, have simply shipped out old computers, or outdated machinery, which were unsuitable in Britain, but could be squeezed for another few years in a less sophisticated environment. Often the Western partner may have embarked on the joint venture simply as a way of keeping a finger on the pulse of Eastern Europe, and may be less committed to expanding operations than the Eastern partners, to whom the joint venture represents their only hope of salvation. A Western partner with a stake of less than 50% may be very frustrated by the different style of management and by his inability to change things. On the other hand, once the Western partner has over 50%, the home partner has, to all intents and purposes, lost control of the operation. The lack of hard currency causes many problems. The prevalence of unreliable suppliers means that manufacturers have to keep some currency available to buy raw material on the world market if necessary. The local investor often wants to take out any profit immediately,

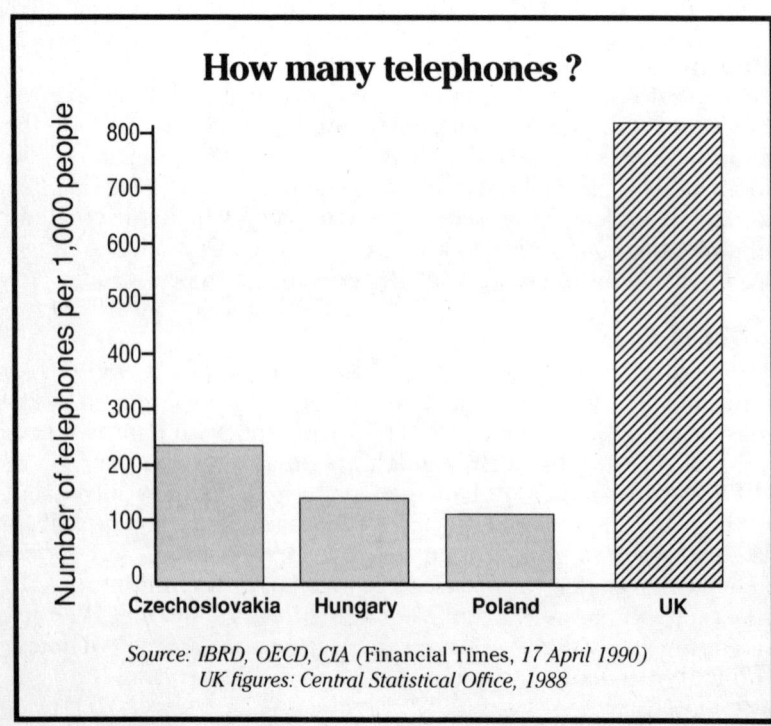

How many telephones ?

Source: IBRD, OECD, CIA (Financial Times, 17 April 1990)
UK figures: Central Statistical Office, 1988

while Western companies are usually happy to re-invest.

Above all, the practical difficulties – getting a telephone, organising office space, dealing with bureaucrats, finding suppliers and buyers – mean that the local partner is crucial in the early stages of a joint venture, but becomes less important once the enterprise is up and running; usually under Western management. It is the fundamental conflict of objectives which jeopardises the success of joint ventures, and means that often they are seen only as a fairly short-term means of getting into a business.

PRIVATISATION

'Privatisation and foreign investment are two sides of the same coin.'

János Martonyi.

As Eastern Europe faced the challenge of transforming itself into a market economy, one of the most pressing issues was how to transform the massive centrally planned economy into an efficient machine. Privatisation was seen as the solution to the greater part of these ills. The problem was how to go about it, how far the process should be taken, how fast it should happen, whether subsidies of inefficient enterprises should be cut before or after privatisation, and so forth.

None of the countries initially had a proper stock exchange, and the local population and enterprises lacked the financial strength to buy shares, or the experience to know how to invest. Vladimir Dlouhy, the Czechoslovak economics minister, pointed out almost immediately after taking up his position that reform would take some time, 'We can hardly privatise all of Czechoslovakian industry very suddenly,' he said (*Financial Times*, 18 January 1990). Hidden debts, poor accounting practices and uncertainty over valuation criteria led to accusations that foreigners were snapping up bargains and depriving the locals of their heritage. Moreover the pre-reformation *nomenklatura* often tried to exploit the privatisation of the enterprise.

The property question was also linked to the question of privatisation. Before privatising assets, ownership must be established. Who should it be – the state, the workers, the directors, the owners who were dispossessed under the communists, or even those dispossessed by the Nazis? The whole issue is a maze of complexity, and East European governments as well as foreign investors, who could involuntarily become involved in this controversial issue, realised that it needed swift resolution .

Privatisation, for some countries, was seen almost as an end in itself, rather than as a way of beginning the repair of the economy. The intrinsic difficulties of the whole process were compounded by the lack of capital and securities markets. Nevertheless, privatisation is a necessary beginning on the road towards shaking out the centrally planned economies.

Czechoslovakia

Throughout the summer of 1990 a debate raged as Václav Klaus, the finance minister, and his colleague Dusan Triska, director of the Office of Management of State Assets, tried to convince the rest of the government and the country to accept a novel method of privatisation. Klaus decided the only way to eliminate state control rapidly, not sell off the country's assets to foreigners and nevertheless overcome the lack of domestic capital in Czechoslovakia, was to issue vouchers to each citizen entitling each individual to a certain share of the country. Klaus testily argued that, 'The voucher system is a short-term mechanism, for changing property rights.' While acknowledging that unemployment and social hardship could result, he felt that these were necessary evils for reform.

It was the long-term effects that his colleagues in government were worried about; President Václav Havel was particularly concerned about the social costs. Vladimir Dlouhy, the economics minister, believed that the enterprises' poor financial situation would negate any benefits, since the voucher system would fail to bring in new capital, and would unnecessarily complicate the issue of ownership. He argued that privatisation was a long-term process. In the end a compromise was reached, and in September 1990 the privatisation plan was finally unveiled. The first stage, the 'small privatisation', would affect state-owned shops and restaurants, returning the underdeveloped service sector to private ownership. Under the second stage, 30–40% of Czechoslovak industry would become joint-stock companies, in other words, companies whose ownership is shared between the private sector and the state, on the way to complete privatisation. In an attempt to cushion the social blow the government would probably retain a minority stake in the largest enterprises. The voucher system is expected only to come into force in three or four years' time, if at all.

Hungary

Hungary is the most advanced of the three countries in its theoretical privatisation programme. This began in 1988 with the new laws on joint ventures and property transformation (see pages 98–

9), and during 1988 and 1989 1,600 companies were set up using state assets. At the beginning of 1990 Janós Martonyi, the privatisation commissioner, helped to establish the State Property Agency, whose brief was to police the privatisation process and ensure against abuses. It was also, if possible, to ensure that firms were in reasonable financial health before putting them on the market. The aim was to privatise 80% of the state's assets, which comprised 90% of the nation's total assets. The task was huge. Britain after all, as one is continually told, took ten years to privatise only 5% of its GDP. The Budapest stock exchange was relaunched with great fanfare in June 1990 on the expectation of large privatisation issues to come. It had been active from 1867 until its closure by the Communists in 1948. In 1983 it began to trade in bonds, and in 1987, in a very limited fashion, in stocks. In June 1990 the exchange was relaunched with a listing of Ibusz, the state travel company.

In July 1990 the overall privatisation plan was finally released. Thirty or forty large companies were to be released onto the market to sink or swim as they could. These would become joint-stock companies, and consisted primarily of hotel chains and chemical and pharmaceutical companies, such as Gedeon Richter. Some 40,000 small companies, mainly in the service sector and ranging from petrol stations to hairdressers, were to be compulsorily sold off. The remaining 600 state companies were to be allowed to decentralise and split into smaller units. This was to take place through public share offers on the local or Viennese stock exchanges, through competitive bidding, or through some kind of employee share ownership. It was suggested that there would be four or five waves of such privatisations per year, each releasing a few per cent of state property. Thus over the years the state's holdings would be reduced to a more manageable figure.

Western investors complained that the process took too long. It was complicated by nationalist overtones among the Hungarian Democratic Forum who, after a few bad experiences, began to worry that foreigners were making off with the family silver. Further complications arose with the Enterprise Councils, made up of 50% workers, 50% managers, which theoretically ran 70% of companies and had to vote themselves out of existence before the change could go ahead.

In an effort to involve the local population and avoid criticisms of selling off the national heritage, a new government credit scheme was launched in September 1990 to facilitate the privatisation of smaller enterprises such as retail, catering and other

services. 'Existence' loans, known as E loans, were available
through a fund set up by the German and Hungarian governments
for Hungarians wishing to participate in the privatisation process.

Meanwhile, companies are carrying out their own privatisations
wherever possible, negotiating directly with foreign investors in
an effort to salvage their companies before the SPA pushes them.

A CASE STUDY

There are many problems involved in this process, and the
following case study is just one among many. Gerbeaud is
Budapest's most famous coffee shop, whose Dobos cake was
once famed throughout Central Europe. Under the
communists the café, founded in 1858, was nationalised and
placed under the care of the state chain Hungarhotels. It was
renamed Vörösmarty café, after the square in which it is
situated, but everyone continued to call it Gerbeaud, and
eventually this was officially acknowledged once more. The
café itself occupies the front of a large building run by the
state-owned Company for Milling and Cereals, which has its
headquarters there. Hungarhotels simply leased the café space.

In December 1989 a Hungarian middleman set up a deal,
apparently under the laws prevailing at the time, between the
director of the Milling Company and a German investor, to
turn the whole building into a hotel or an office block. The
German was to take 75% of the profits since he would have to
supply the investment required to renovate and convert the
building, and he would then own 50%. The middleman would
be rewarded with 5% of the new company, the Milling
Company would own the remaining 45%, and the manager
of the Milling Company would take his place on the board of
the new company. The café itself was offered the simple choice
either of being renovated and then sharing the profits with the
new company, or of being renovated and then paying an
increased rent. Public outcry ensued that, once again, the
national heritage was being sold off cheaply to foreigners. An
opposition MP from the Alliance of Free Democrats then
became involved, claiming that the building had been
ridiculously undervalued, given its position and condition.

Basically no one seemed to know if the Milling Company
really owned the building and therefore had the right to sell
it. No one knew who was to get the money from the sale – the
Milling Company or the state? Who would select the valuers
of the building, and what criteria would they use to determine

the valuation? Who would prosecute if there were problems? In this particular case it was the opposition party which initiated proceedings, but this in itself caused extra problems and politicised the debate. Equally, another question mark could be raised over the identity of the judges themselves, whom many see as being ex-communists and therefore suspect. Finally there was the sheer inexperience and naivety of all concerned. Several court cases ensued over the valuation and the contracts, and at the time of writing, nearly a year after the initial contract, the matter has still not been resolved.

This is, of course, an extreme case, but nevertheless it indicates some of the pitfalls involved in privatisation. Another sale which fell foul of the law was that of the whole chain of Hungarhotels itself. Initially sold to a Swedish-Dutch investment group, the sale was cancelled due to similar uncertainties, and Hungarhotels was relaunched for privatisation in September 1990. The sale of the lighting manufacturer, Tungsram, also upset local opinion. This was bought by the Austrian bank, Girozentrale, for $120 million and resold three weeks later for $150 million to General Electric of the United States. The Hungarians were furious, but also began to realise the value of their assets.

As the new valuation rules came into operation in late 1990, the State Property Agency began to play a more active role. Companies could be privatised in three ways. The first was by official selection by the SPA. The second was by 'spontaneous' privatisation whereby the managers took the initiative. The final method was by a form of corporate raid. An investor would approach the SPA with a bid. Within thirty days the SPA would in each case specify the amount of local and foreign ownership it would be prepared to accept, along with any other conditions. It would also look for any counter-bids. The investor then had another thirty to ninety days in which to make a final bid. Meanwhile, the company must organise an audit and transform itself into a joint-stock company. The theory was deceptively simple, but only experience would reveal the flaws.

Poland

As early as 1989 Krzysztof Lis had been appointed minister for privatisation, but the whole issue remained unclear until the passing of the Privatisation Bill in mid 1990. The debate raged over how to prevent the *nomenklatura* from simply featherbedding their new careers, and how to permit worker ownership without restricting new owners to short-term policies geared only to preventing redundancies. How could one ensure that the Polish population was not deprived of its heritage, while acknowledging that personal savings would only be enough to buy less than 10% of what would become available? If workers were limited only to shares in their own enterprises, then this would, it was argued, unfairly penalise bureaucrats and those in unsuccessful enterprises. The smaller enterprises were easier to reorganise. By August 1990 at least 15,000 shops had been privatised, bringing to 25% the number of privately run retail outlets[4]. It was the larger industries and organisations that posed the problem.

By April 1990 the finance minister, Leszek Balcerowicz, was on his seventeenth draft of the Privatisation Bill, and political tension began to mount. As in Hungary, a couple of highly publicised abuses, where members of the previous government and managers of large enterprises profitably 'privatised' their companies, only increased the pressure. Meanwhile, Western companies, such as British accountancy firms and merchant banks, were called in to prepare plans for future privatisation of targeted industries. Eventually an estimated 9,000 enterprises would be privatised.

Finally in July 1990, after a delay which Lech Walesa strongly criticised for the opportunities it had provided to the unscrupulous, the necessary legislation was passed by 328 votes to 2, indicating the eventual near-unanimity after the months of hesitation. There was now a framework to transfer state-owned industries to the private sector. A Ministry for Property Transformation was established under Waldemar Kuczynski, parallel to the existing Foreign Investment Agency. Its responsibilities included selecting relatively profitable enterprises, or receiving suggestions from the enterprises themselves, for privatisation. It was also to help prepare the enterprises, advising them on valuations, drawing up accounts and so on. Once selected, companies would then become joint-stock companies, still state-owned, probably by the Treasury, and within two years shares would be sold off either through auction, public offer or negotiated purchase. Up to 10% foreign ownership was permitted, but this restriction could probably be side-stepped by using the joint-venture legislation which permitted up to 100%.

Workers could buy up to 20% of the shares in their own companies at the preferential rate of half the market price. In this way 7,600 enterprises were to be transformed into limited corporations. Each adult Pole is also to receive a privatisation bond or voucher entitling him to a share in his country's assets, but at the time of writing the details have yet to be decided. Shares in the first five enterprises were successfully launched in December 1990.

IMPORT/EXPORT

Import/export is one of the areas which has seen the greatest change since the revolutions of 1989.

Czechoslovakia

In Czechoslovakia virtually all imports and exports used to be carried out by the fifty-four Foreign Trade Organisations, controlled by the Federal Ministry of Foreign Trade. Under the old laws, trade was completely nationalised, and official authorisation, only available from the Foreign Trade Ministry, was necessary to engage in foreign trade. There was a different Foreign Trade Organisations for every possible branch of commercial activity. Thus, Motokov dealt with the car trade, Centrotex with textiles, Jablonex with costume jewellery and so on. Both imports and exports passed through these FTOs, so anyone wanting to sell in Czechoslovakia had to contact the appropriate FTO, sending catalogues, price lists and whatever, and then follow up usually with a visit, again organised through the FTO. Likewise, if the foreign businessman wanted to buy, he contacted the FTO, who arranged viewing, contracts, quotas and delivery dates.

Under reforms initiated in 1988, which came into force in January 1990, an attempt was made to restructure some of the FTOs, so that leading companies and producers were actually merged with their FTO. In addition, some state companies could opt out of using their FTO and deal directly with foreign exporters. In the short term this probably means that the larger and more competent companies will become independent, while the smaller and less efficient ones will remain under the protective umbrella of their FTO. In the long term the future of the FTOs is uncertain.

Centrotex, the FTO dealing with the textile industry, provides a stark illustration of the problems now faced by the FTOs. It occupies a huge office block in Prague and employs 1,200 people. The place is a labyrinth of materials, with Aladdin's caves of dull-looking corduroys, haphazardly piled carpets and old-fashioned trilbies on display in specialised locked rooms opening off long corridors. By June 1990 about ten factories had already opted out from their representation. Before the reforms Centrotex had a two-person public relations department, one of whom spoke no language other than Czech and was therefore redundant in an organisation dealing exclusively with foreign trade. An organisation spokeswoman thought Centrotex might eventually be reduced to 600 staff. At best, drastic staff cuts will have to be made in state bureaucratic areas such as the FTOs, which have always been overmanned and bureaucratic. At worst, FTOs will be abolished altogether as they become completely redundant.

In January 1990, Andrej Barcak, minister of foreign trade and former executive of Motokov, the FTO for the car industry, said, 'I might concede the monopoly of foreign trade in consumer goods and in some other specific instances, but not across the board and certainly not in the engineering industry.' (*Financial Times*, 25 January 1990.) Mr Barcak was ousted as minister of foreign trade five months later.

In July 1990 a decree was passed designed to facilitate the establishment and operation of commercial representations of foreign companies. According to this decree, foreign firms, through their agents, were finally permitted to advertise and conclude agreements with registered Czechoslovak companies, something which had previously passed through the FTOs. Enterprises are now permitted to import directly to cater for their own needs, and one can assume that the more able companies will organise their own suppliers and clients, while the less able go to the wall. Companies wanting to trade abroad can now do so, but they must first register a deposit of 20,000 crowns ($830) security. Enterprises can now retain a proportion of their export earnings, instead of – as previously – feeding it back into the system, so companies now have an incentive to organise their own contracts.

However, the FTOs are still influential and obviously retain major advantages in that they already have contacts both locally and with the West, and expertise in foreign trade, though under very different conditions. They will fight to retain their influence.

Major import and export programmes will, at least in the short term, still be determined centrally and will therefore be organised through the relevant FTO. The total lack of experience of the companies will also encourage them to continue trading through their FTO initially. As Helena Felix of Aquascutum, which has been trading in Czechoslovakia for twenty years, said, 'They want to be independent, but I think they don't necessarily understand how difficult the world is outside.'

The foreign company wishing to trade in Czechoslovakia should therefore combine continued trading through the FTO with direct approaches to the enterprises concerned. According to Department of Trade and Industry (DTI) advice, 'personal visits to the market are essential'. This still remains good advice, especially in a country which has problems with telephones and post.

Hungary

In Hungary all production enterprises have been entitled to foreign trading rights since 1988, increasing the number of registered enterprises which could undertake foreign trade ten-fold. The proportion of goods subject to permit requirements was also eased, so that nearly three-quarters of items required no licence.

Hungarian FTOs are in a much weaker position than Czech ones, and their monopoly has been eroded in recent years, though smaller enterprises tend to rely on them still. Otherwise individual contacts with companies are necessary. From January 1991, companies can pay in local currency for their imports.

Apart from the lack of hard currency, export and import conditions in Hungary have much in common with usual trade conditions in the rest of Europe.

Poland

In Poland, too, foreign trade was a state monopoly organised through the Foreign Trade Enterprises (Przedsiębiorstwa Handlu Zagranicznego, PHZ) in similar fashion to the Czechoslovak FTOs. This system is now open to competition as the Foreign Trade Enterprises have lost their monopolies. All enterprises can now carry out foreign trade without express permission, though Poland still has about 100 remaining PHZs.

COUNTER-TRADE

The shortage of hard currency in Eastern Europe means that counter-trade and barter are issues which face most companies at some time. It is estimated that over 25% of Comecon/Western trade was carried out in this fashion. The East European Trade Council defines counter-trade as meaning, 'all forms of barter, counter-purchase, compensation trading, offset, buy-back and switch dealing.' Short of borrowing more money, using Western loans or parting with their hard-earned export profits, Eastern European governments and enterprises have little choice but to offer barter or counter-trade proposals. Thus Poland, already heavily in debt, or Czechoslovakia, reluctant to fall into the same trap, will offer counter-trade, saving valuable currency and encouraging trade in other areas. In Hungary, counter-trade has been significant since the early 1970s, when serious trading began but hard currency was in short supply.

Trade in chemical and manufactured products, machinery, equipment and investment goods may all be subject to counter-trade pressure. A good deal of haggling goes on in the early stages to reduce the percentage of the deal acceptable in kind, and to specify the kind of goods. Nevertheless, the East European Trade Council believes that counter-trade is not an unsurmountable obstacle and should not be rejected out of hand.

As decentralisation begins to become a reality, rather than merely a policy, counter-trade becomes harder to organise, since there is no longer a central planner to organise the exchange of widgets for bananas, or whatever. Banana importers and widget exporters will in future be run as separate companies.

The Hungarian and Polish governments now strongly encourage producers to improve their goods, the aim being that they should be of adequate quality to sell in their own right. One of the main problems for Western businesses lies in finding a possible barter item, reliably delivered, of good quality, and above all, re-saleable. Of course, it helps if the goods received are in the same field of business, since knowledge of the product is, to say the least, helpful. Avon Cosmetics, for instance, which started direct selling in Hungary in 1990, was forced to use or export a certain quantity of Hungarian products in return for import licences to bring in their own products. Eventually they found they could use certain items within their own field – pump sprays for fragrance bottles, print material for their brochures, Christmas decorations for seasonal sales. This meant the counter-trade was feasible. Hungary in particular offers services such as printing as counter-trade.

A similar type of barter deal was set up between Polish Television and Walt Disney. In return for the rights to show Disney films, the Polish broadcaster offered the film distributors all the advertising time within the shows to sell on to international companies.

The switch within Comecon countries from rouble to dollar accounting will probably increase the pressure to organise counter-trade. Tungsram, the Hungarian light-bulb manufacturer bought by the US company General Electric, accepted 2,000 Lada cars from the Soviet Union in return for industrial robots in 1990. Harry Codd, chief executive of Ganz-Hunslet, the Anglo-Hungarian train manufacturer, suddenly found himself devising counter-trade and supply agreements to permit the Soviet Union to supply certain parts of the locomotives which would then be fitted into the Hungarian units and sold back to the Soviet Union. Codd noted, 'There are some quite ingenious accountancy methods required.' Needless to say, the process is very time-consuming.[5]

CHAPTER 6

SOURCES OF AID AND BRITAIN'S RESPONSE

Even before the 'revolutions' of 1989, the European Community's attitude towards Eastern Europe had been evolving. The EC and Comecon had issued a joint declaration in June 1988 declaring their intention 'to develop co-operation'. A few months later an agreement was signed between the Community and Hungary whereby quantitative restrictions on imports were to be lifted by 1995. The following year, in September 1989, a similar agreement was signed with Poland, and these concessions were brought forward to January 1990 in the light of the political reforms which had taken place. In August 1989 the Group of 24 or G24 (consisting of the twelve EC members, six European Free Trade Association [EFTA] members, and the United States, Japan, Canada, Turkey, New Zealand and Australia) agreed on a programme of economic support for Eastern Europe. It came to be known as PHARE – Poland and Hungary: Assistance for Economic Restructuring – although barely six months later it was extended to include Czechoslovakia, Romania (later suspended as doubts over the democratic nature of the new government arose), Bulgaria and East Germany (until unification). The five main areas of PHARE's activities are: food aid and restructuring of agriculture; access to Western markets for East European goods; promotion of investment; professional and vocational training and environmental assistance. Poland in particular has been given considerable food aid. PHARE has become the main channel for Western aid to the East.

Companies interested in participating in PHARE should contact the relevant department of the European Commission (see page 137 for addresses). Projects must be approved by the appropriate East European country first, and then by the management committee of the member states in Brussels. Training is considered the single most important area for investment, and this has been sub-divided into: 'on-the-job industrial training linked to industrial restructuring, export market research, management courses and financial services training.' Environmental protection is another top priority, the aim being to reduce pollution in industrial areas. In the agricultural sector the stated aim is to encourage private farming by supplying training, equipment and technology. Industrial restructuring requires technology, capital and skills, and the EC, 'will initiate and financially support sectoral studies as a basis for future actions.'

Even before Czechoslovakia's 'velvet revolution' broke out, Poland and Hungary had been given or pledged over 700 million ecu (£500 million) in aid, either through the EC budget or bilaterally. The European Investment Bank had been authorised to make loans of 1 billion ecu (£729 million) in project loans to Poland and Hungary pending the formation of a special East European bank. A 'stabilisation fund' of $1 billion was planned for Poland to foster confidence in the zloty, and a similar-sized bridging loan was organised for Hungary. Not for nothing was the World Bank's first permanent office in Eastern Europe opened in Warsaw in 1990.

Other sources of aid include: the International Finance Corporation (IFC), an arm of the World Bank, set up to promote private sector investment in developing countries; the United Nations Industrial Development Organisation in Vienna; the International Bank for Reconstruction and Development, also part of the World Bank, with similar aims to those of the IFC[1].

The European Council summit in Strasbourg in December 1989 decided on further initiatives. The most important of these was the implementation of one of President Mitterand's ideas; the creation of a European Bank for Reconstruction and Development (BERD or EBRD) whose founding statutes were signed in May 1990. The total capital of this new bank was to be 10 billion ecu (£7.4 billion), about half of which was to be supplied by Community members. Forty-two partners took smaller shares, among which the United States, Japan, EFTA, the European Investment Bank and the Soviet Union were pre-eminent. Initial discussions centred on the location of the bank – eventually conceded to London, the identity of the first president – finally conferred on Jacques Attali, Mitterand's financial adviser, and the denomination of the bank's capital, which fluctuated between ecu and dollars.

The BERD was established to fund private and public sector projects in all fields in Eastern Europe. Theoretically the bank would cover the roles of merchant bank and regional development agency. It could lend to governments, local banks, state enterprises and the private sector, and could take a direct stake in businesses if necessary. Its main role is to be an investment catalyst, especially by providing investment guarantees to encourage Western private investors.

Meanwhile aid was also allocated directly by the European Commission and the United States. By November 1989 the Commission had allocated about 1 billion ecus (£729 million) for Poland and half as much for Hungary[2]. Poland, for example, received grants, loans and debt relief from individual industrialised countries, from the European Investment Bank, as well as from various export credit agencies and international organisations. As the full implications of Eastern Europe's impact on the European Community's economy become clearer, the EC may be less enthusiastic about Hungarian farm produce or cheap Polish labour. A British Parliamentary Select Committee reviewing the situation in July 1990 commented drily, 'Whether Western governments have sufficient public resources to affect materially the prospects of the majority of East European countries is open to doubt.'

The British government does not provide grants or loans to companies wishing to do business with Eastern Europe. It is, however, publicly supportive and some incentives are available. Two schemes not specific to Eastern Europe are run by the Department of Trade and Industry (DTI). The first is the 'Hands on Training Scheme for Overseas Decision Makers', dubbed HOTS, which was created to help with management training. Companies propose candidates and draw up a training programme for them which will emphasise British technology, management and production methods. If the DTI can be convinced that the training, 'would bring significant benefits both to the company and to wider British industry,' then it will contribute up to 50% of the cost[3].

The second scheme is the Overseas Project Fund which aims to encourage British companies 'to pursue marginal projects which they would not otherwise pursue'. It exists to support bidding and feasibility studies and hopes 'to increase the number of contracts the UK can go after and win'. Only contracts with a UK content of £50 million or over are eligible. Priority sectors include construction, consultancy, design, engineering and training.

The highest profile government scheme is the Know-How Fund. This was announced in June 1989, when General Jaruzelski was visiting Britain after the Polish elections which first brought Solidarity to power. Initially set at £25 million over five years for Poland alone, it was doubled in November when Walesa visited

Britain. In the spring of 1990 it was further extended by £25 million to cover first Hungary, and subsequently the German Democratic Republic (until reunification) and Czechoslovakia. The fund is run by the Joint Assistance Unit at the Foreign and Commonwealth Office and is advised by a committee of politicians, businessmen, trade unionists and journalists.

The fund received a great deal of criticism in its early months. Not only was it 'ludicrously inadequate to the task,' according to the *Guardian* (March 1990), but a high proportion of projects funded seemed to be made up of seminars on topics such as parliamentary procedure, or feasibility studies on relatively eso-teric projects, such as fractionation of blood products. The initial opinion of businessmen and academics was that the Know-How Fund was unsuccessful. Yochanan Altman of Cranfield School of Management commented on the fund's first year of activity: 'Look at the list of Know-How and you want to jump out of the window. It's a very big miss indeed.' Jo Malins of Hunslet Holdings, which had just bought Ganz in Budapest reported in June 1990 that the British government had provided very little help at all during his Hungarian negotiations. In the first months the department assigned the task of co-ordinating the fund was overwhelmed with the sheer amount of work. Towards the end of 1990, however, initial organisational problems were gradually ironed out and the fund began to make a more positive contribution.

For Poland, priority sectors are considered to be industrial restructuring, and banking and financial services, though agri-culture, tourism, energy and management training are also of considerable importance. The Confederation of British Industry has linked up with the British Council to provide training in the UK for around 1,400 Polish managers. For Hungary, priority sectors are privatisation, financial services, management training, public administration retraining and the encouragement of small enterprises.

The Know-How Fund looks favourably on 'Pre-Investment Feasibility Studies', which it could partially fund in order to encourage UK businesses to investigate long-term investment in Eastern Europe. It could also be used to fund management training for joint-venture partners. Long-term benefits, of course, are expected. Costain Engineering, for instance, invited several structural engineers from Prochem in Poland to work with them in Britain for several months. One of these engineers, Jaroslaw Piotrowski, hoped to learn about computer networks and 'organ-isational systems', while Bob Boland of Costain hoped to improve his company's trading relationship and strengthen international links: 'I hope Polish engineers that have worked with us will see us as a source of information and help for projects that need to be undertaken there in the future.' Harry Codd of Ganz-Hunslet commented that government aid was not really the point. 'The best kind of British aid is to place orders,' he said.

British business in Czechoslovakia has been limited, according to Stephen Holby, export finance manager of Barclays Bank, to 'specialists and exceptions'. By March 1990 Britain was only involved in 48 out of 900 joint ventures in Hungary. A survey carried out by an executive search company in February 1990 confirmed that most British managers believed companies were showing insufficient initiative and experience in approaching East European markets.

It is quite possible that by the time Eastern Europe provides an attractive hard currency market, most initial opportunities will have been taken by competitors from other countries, especially Germany and Austria. Once Eastern Europe's economy is on its feet moreover, it will become a competitor, not just 'an opportunity', and if British businessmen have not foreseen this they will be increasingly marginalised on the periphery of the continent. John Thorley of the National Sheep Association commented in June 1990: 'A matter of concern is Eastern Europe. Who would have thought the Eastern Bloc would have given anything to worry about in competitive terms.' What is true for sheep may soon prove to be true for most British businesses!

CHAPTER 7

PRACTICALITIES

This section attempts to provide some helpful hints to those attempting to do business in Eastern Europe, perhaps for the first time. It is by no means an exhaustive list, but offers some tips which may shorten a somewhat tortuous path for Western businessmen. When no particular country is specified, this indicates that the information is applicable to Hungary, Poland and Czechoslovakia. Relevant addresses can be found in Chapter 8.

ACCOMMODATION

Throughout the Eastern European capitals, houses and flats for rental are difficult to find, reflecting a lack of investment over the years. Prague is a particular blackspot for any accommodation.

In Budapest PK (Pénzintézeti Központ, an agency run by the Central Corporation of Banking Companies) helps foreign managers to find accommodation, in return for 10% of what are already higher than local rental costs. Furthermore, rents are not usually fixed, must be paid for in convertible currency and have a nasty tendency to rise sharply with inflation. The maximum lease for a house or flat is thirty years.

Dispservice in Poland performs a similar function to Hungary's PK, by arranging flats and villas for Western businessmen. (See also Office Space, page 132 Property, page 133.)

ACCOUNTANCY

A Western businessman faced with a set of Eastern European accounts will find a sheaf of papers quite different from those he is used to handling. In the past, accountants prepared their books to comply with five-year plans, not to show the financial health of an enterprise. If the businessman is using them to evaluate the profitability of a company in which he hopes to invest, he must be aware of their shortcomings. If they are being produced by the accounts department of a company in which he has already invested, say as a partner in a joint venture, then he must rapidly institute a workable management accounting system, which will also necessitate retraining the locally employed accountants.

Under the centrally planned economies, accounts were target, not profit orientated. Audits were prepared for statistical and fiscal purposes, simply to establish the production achieved by an enterprise, while the notion of profitability fell by the wayside. The information amassed was probably accurate in its own way, but several crucial factors never made it to the balance sheets. As David Harrison of Tungsram in Hungary told the *Financial Times*, 'There's lots of data but it's not decision-making data.' Depreciation or appreciation of assets was ignored. The effects of inflation were overlooked. Only cash transactions were considered, while money owed was disregarded. Huge debts were shifted between state enterprises. Barter deals complicated the books. Bankruptcy was an impossibility. The unreliability of supplies and distribution meant that companies bought stock whenever it became available, and then stored vast quantities of materials. Prices themselves were fixed and therefore provided an unreliable factor in determining the health of a company. Then, as subsidies were slashed, future sales and prices became unpredictable. Add to all this the fact that there is little computerisation and it is clear that the whole area requires considerable attention.

There are, unfortunately, very few people capable of providing this attention. *Accountancy* magazine (August 1990) estimated that there were perhaps only fifty accountants in Czechoslovakia capable of carrying out an effective audit, although since 1988 joint-venture companies with foreign investment were obliged to employ two auditors, and from May 1990 this requirement was extended to domestic share companies. This led to calls to re-establish the Czechoslovak Union of Accountants. In the meantime there is a severe shortage of native accountants.

Hungary as usual is further advanced. Western companies moved in to Budapest *en masse* in 1988, initially with small investments. They have been training local staff, and with the development of the financial market, concepts of Western accounting are becoming more familiar. Nevertheless, there are still skills to be learnt by local accountants, ranging from preparing income statements through simple balance sheets to annual reports.

The Polish Association of Accountants was founded in 1907 and represented all qualified accountants in the country. There are about 120,000 'technician members' and 10,000 fully qualified accountants, who can conduct audits. This latter group renamed itself the National Board of Chartered Accountants of Poland, and in 1989 was admitted to membership of the International Accounting Standards Committee. With the passing of the Foreign

Investment Act in 1988 (see page 99) an independent audit became necessary for all companies with foreign participation, but existing joint ventures with Western capital could use Western standards. Finally, new rules drafted in March 1990 came into force on 1 January 1991 which specify uniform practices which take account of international accounting standards, and aim to comply with the European Community's Fourth Directive. Accounts must, however, be kept in Polish.

Until local accountants gain experience of the new methods this will be an area where they will need training and considerable initial advice from the West, unless companies are willing to resort to expensive outside consultation.

ADVERTISING

This is an underdeveloped and fast changing sector. (See pages 70–2.)

In Czechoslovakia, CTK Made-In used to be the main advertising agency, but the field is now open to all comers. *Rudé Pravo* is the newspaper with the largest circulation, but with press deregulation media is booming. The technical press is also widely read though drably presented. New scientific developments can also be publicised through the Czechoslovak Scientific-Technical Society (CSVTS). A recent change is advertising on television. An estimated 25% of the country's total trade contracts are signed at the main trade fairs, so this is an important means of establishing a presence in the market. (See also Trade Fairs, page 135.)

It is a good idea to remember that Slovaks are sensitive about their language, so it may be worth printing a separate Slovakian language brochure if the main market is expected to be Slovakia.

Hungary's two large state agencies are Hungexpo and Mahir. State technical information centres can be helpful on a professional level. Advertising for cigarettes and alcohol is prohibited.

In Poland the Chamber of Foreign Trade has a promotions department which provides advice. The main agency used to be AGPOL, but other independent agencies are now moving into the market.

COMMUNICATIONS

During the last forty years investment in telecommunications fell far behind Western standards. Czechoslovakia has only twenty-five telephones per 100 population, Hungary fifteen and Poland only thirteen. In order to catch up, Hungary estimates it must spend £4 billion. Poland plans to spend £8 billion during the 1990s.

As well as modernising the main telephone networks, several companies have been looking at the mobile telephone networks. In December 1990 a cellular telephone network came into operation in Hungary, and Czechoslovakia is expected to have a system operational by mid 1991. Poland will not be far behind. This should ease some problems for Western businessmen.

Telex machines are freely available in Czechoslovakia once an office has been established. Western businessmen will therefore have to readapt their method of communication, since although fax machines can be purchased for hard currency, the proper paper is difficult to obtain, and a telephone line harder still.

In Poland public telephones require special tokens which can be purchased in 'Ruch' kiosks. A public fax service is available in Warsaw at the main post office. In general, communications are notoriously difficult, in some areas impossible when it rains, and crossed lines frequent. A recent survey carried out by MBA graduates at Cranfield School of Management uncovered a new occupational hazard, known as 'Warsaw finger', which they diagnosed as an inflammation caused by repetitive telephone dialling.[1]

DISTRIBUTION

In the past this was a major problem due to supply shortages, unreliable quality of the means of transport and a lack of both staff motivation and market pressure. If these problems can be resolved, distribution difficulties should be eased, though the poor road and rail networks will continue to provide an obstacle.

EMPLOYEES

Local staff: Average salaries for mid 1990 in Czechoslovakia stood around 7,000 crowns ($290) per month for a secretary, 3,300 crowns ($140) for an unskilled worker and 20,000 crowns ($840) for a manager. About 12% goes on taxes. Salaries are negotiated individually with employees, very few of whom have private bank accounts and so expect to be paid in cash.

In Hungary, in August 1990, monthly wages were approximately 50,000 forints ($750) for a manager, 20,000 forints ($300) for a secretary, and 10,000 forints ($150) for unskilled workers, but inflation has pushed these up rapidly. Minimum wage from September 1990 was set at 5,000 forints ($85). Western companies pay a 43% wage tax as the social security contribution for each local employee. It is advisable for Western employers to offer higher salaries than other employers (which would still be very low) so that they can insist that employees do not take on a second job; most Hungarians need the extra income to make ends meet.

Average salaries in Poland in mid 1990 were approximately $200 a month for a secretary and $500 for a manager. On 1 September 1990 the new minimum monthly wage was set at 368,000 zloty ($40). Thirty eight percent is paid directly to social security. The Office of Employment in Warsaw must be notified of all local employees.

Motivation can be immeasurably improved by offering hard-currency bonuses. Training is also highly valued. The threat of large-scale unemployment is likely to favour employers in their search for staff loyalty, although there will still be a shortage of English-speakers with the necessary skills.

Foreign staff: In a survey carried out by Merton Associates and Transearch International in February 1990, financial reward was cited by managers as the most important factor in deciding whether or not to accept postings in Eastern Europe. Good accommodation and high quality medical services were the predominant social and domestic priorities[2]. In Hungary Western employees of joint ventures are exempt from income tax and social insurance payments. Fifty per cent of net income can be transferred into hard currency and repatriated.

ETIQUETTE
Continental European manners are observed throughout Eastern Europe. People greet on entering small shops, and shake hands when meeting and leaving. In Poland, women should not shake hands vigorously in case their hand is about to be kissed!

FINANCIAL AND LEGAL
Eastern Europe's financial and legal infrastructure is in the same underdeveloped state as its transport and communications networks. Under the communist economy the banks, for instance, existed only to funnel credit into state enterprises on orders from central government as they received orders from other departments, also within central government.

Czechoslovakia
Czechoslovakia initiated a banking reform on 1 January 1990 which aimed at restructuring the system by creating two tiers. The State Bank (Statni Banka) ceased commercial activities to concentrate on implementing state policy. The main commercial bank, especially for foreign investors, became the Ceskoslovenska

Obchodni Banka, or Commercial Bank. It is responsible for all transfers of foreign currency, export/import payments and other international dealings. The Investicni Banka run by the Ministry of Finance provides the link between Western companies and the government. It also has other semi-governmental functions, and is likely to grow in importance as Czechoslovakia's Western contacts expand. Several foreign banks, led by the Austrians and the Swiss have already set up branches in Czechoslovakia.

The Czech currency, the crown or koruna, became internally convertible on 1 January 1991. The black market remained fairly healthy, although severe penalties were imposed for locals, with deportation threatened for Western businessmen caught breaking the law. The State Bank estimated that it had lost about $200 million in 1990 due to black market transactions[3]. Unwary tourists used to be trapped at the border by the exchange regulations, unable to take out their crowns, or to change them or to spend them on anything.

Foreign Trade Organisations and joint ventures (see Chapter 5) can transfer money outside the country without specific authorisation, but all other transfers require Finance Ministry permission. Thirty per cent of foreign currency profits must be offered to Czech banks for conversion, presumably at unfavourable rates.

Income tax amounts to 20% of taxable income up to 20,000 crowns ($830), after which the rate rises to 40%, but exceptions are frequently made. Wages tax generally amounts to 50% of the total wages paid, but again exceptions are common. The foreign partner in a joint-venture company generally pays a tax on dividends at the rate of 25%. Although negotiations are progressing there is still no double taxation treaty between the United Kingdom and Czechoslovakia. Official sources in Czechoslovakia therefore recommend that the British partner invest in an Austrian or Cypriot company which would then carry out the investment in the joint venture. This situation will probably change in the near future, and investors should check how it applies to them.

An Investment Promotion and Protection Agreement between the United Kingdom and Czechoslovakia was signed in July 1990. It provides safeguards for investors in Czechoslovakia in the event of appropriation of assets. The agreement may also lead to greater possibilities for repatriation of profits.

Hungary
On 1 January 1987 the Hungarian banking system was reor-

ganised into a two-tier system with the National Bank acting as the central bank responsible for formulating and executing economic policy. Companies were given a free choice of bank, and in 1989 individual clients were allowed to place savings deposits with the commercial banks. One of the main changes as far as Western investors were concerned was the relaxation of the National Bank's monopoly over foreign transactions, though it continued to play the leading role in the application of government policy, and its directives were binding on other banks. The Hungarian Foreign Trade Bank used to have a privileged position, but as Hungary privatised its banks this no longer held true. Foreign banks opened branches during the 1980s usually as joint ventures with local institutions, but during 1990 international banks began to open wholly owned branches.

The Hungarian forint is not yet convertible, but Ferenc Rabár, the day after his appointment as finance minister in March 1990, promised this would happen 'some time between the end of 1991 and the middle of 1992.' Foreign investors can, however, transfer abroad in the currency of the original investment their profits and any proceeds of the sale of shares.

Personal taxation and VAT were introduced in 1988. In terms of individual taxation, anyone staying in Hungary for over 182 days a year becomes eligible for Hungarian taxation. In order to encourage foreign investment there are very favourable tax benefits for joint ventures. Any joint venture with up to 20% foreign equity can be eligible for tax exemptions for up to five years. This led to local hostility and justified complaints about preferential treatment for foreigners, and the system is to be reviewed in the near future. It will, however, 'retain and extend the system of encouraging enterprise for next year as well,' according to Katalin Botos of the Ministry of Finance.

The standard rate for company taxation has been reduced from 50% to 40% (less for incomes below 3 million forints, $45,000). Priority sectors, including computers, telecommunications, agriculture and food processing machinery, pharmaceuticals and tourism, can be exempted from taxation for up to five years, and even then only pay 16%. Hungary has double taxation treaties with all the main countries in Western Europe including Britain (1979). There is also a UK-Hungarian Bilateral Investment Promotion and Protection Agreement, and separate insurance can be obtained through the Export Credits Guarantee Department.

The opening of the Budapest stock exchange provided a psychological boost to the Hungarian financial market. Several investment funds were then established, expressly aimed at the Hungarian market. The First Hungary Fund saw itself as a 'country growth fund', and focused on small- and medium-sized private companies, existing joint ventures and recently privatised enterprises. It was founded by the Hungarian National Bank, the International Finance Corporation and two Hungarian emigrés, Andrew Sarlos and George Soros, and raised an initial $80 million. It was quickly followed by the Hungarian Investment Corporation, organised by British investment manager John Govett, which was oversubscribed at $100 million. The Hungarian Investment Corporation aimed to invest primarily in large companies requiring an investment outlay of $5 million, but initially found few companies large enough to be interesting outside the manufacturing sector, with all its associated problems. Other funds included the Central European Development Corporation, which included among its capital contributors Ronald Lauder, chief executive of Estée Lauder, herself of Hungarian origin, and Merrill Lynch's Austro-Hungary Fund.

The Hungarian enterprises are usually looking for more active partners who would help plan strategy, train staff or supply technology, and not just provide money. The stock market is restricted and the size of Hungarian companies in general very small, so these funds have not initially been fully stretched. As Lajos Bokros, the exchange president, told Mrs Thatcher when she visited the exchange in September 1990: 'Small is beautiful.'

Poland

Nine new commercial banks were opened during 1988, but in spite of these efforts to de-monopolise and improve services, Poland's banking system remained in a primitive state. For customers this means that a cheque could take a month to clear, money could take three weeks to transfer, and the simplest transaction may mean standing in a queue for over an hour. Computer networks are restricted by the outdated telephone system. Credit cards are virtually unknown outside the main tourist sites, although American Express announced it had got a licence to operate in Poland from August 1990.

The Narodowy Bank Polski is the central bank, but the main bank for foreign investors is the Bank Handlowy, or Commercial Bank, which deals with all foreign trade matters. Leading Western Central Banks, including the United States Federal Reserve, the Bundesbank and the Bank of England, were brought in to advise the Polish government[4]. As a result of the government's austerity programme in early 1990, the zloty is convertible.

The free-enterprise atmosphere prevailing in Poland during 1990 led to its first major banking scandal. Lech Grobelny, a photographer who converted his automatic photo booths into hard-currency kiosks, opened the BKO, the private Safe Savings Bank, offering 180% interest on one year's deposit, and amassed a fortune estimated at around $2 million. In June 1990 he disappeared, with the money of 10,000 investors, and his bank crashed amid rumours that he was in South Africa or Latin America. The Poles began to appreciate the dark side of deregulation.

Corporate income tax exemptions are offered in priority sectors which include the agro-processing industry, pharmaceuticals and medical equipment, the chemical industry, environmental protection, 'modern technologies', telecommunications, electronics, tourism, printing and office-automation equipment. Britain has a bilateral agreement to avoid double taxation. In corporations where the foreign party holds a minimum of 10% of votes, the tax on the dividend is 5%; in all other cases it is 15%. VAT is to be introduced in the near future.

At the time of writing, Poland has no stock exchange, and international consultants from the OECD have recommended that the country concentrate on banking reform and leave the establishment of the stock exchange until the economy is at a more advanced state. Meanwhile, after a fifty-year gap, the Polish Press Agency has begun to publish a 'stock exchange service'. The government hopes to start some kind of limited stock exchange in 1991, with the help of the Paris Bourse, but in the absence of any proper investment banks, pension funds, substantial savings or an understanding of the functioning of an exchange, it will probably be, like Hungary's, of rather limited importance in the short term.

HOTELS

Hotel rooms are very difficult to reserve in Czechoslovakia, and it may require a little personal attention to the manager, in the form of a bottle of whisky, for example, to obtain one. Prague is a particular black spot, and trade-fair time in Brno and Bratislava also presents problems. Some far-sighted companies even reserve their accommodation a year in advance.

In Budapest there are similar problems at trade-fair time, though the situation is not so acute for the rest of the year, and the standard of hotel is superior.

Hotel space in Warsaw has, in the last year, become much easier to find than in the other capitals.

INFORMATION

The Foreign Trade Organisation for the relevant sector should be consulted. The Department of Trade and Industry's East European desks are a principal source of information.

The Czechoslovak Chamber of Commerce in Prague is also a major source. It produces handbooks and journals which are frequently updated, for example on the latest commercial laws. It is also compiling a data base of enterprises interested in joint ventures in various sectors. The Czechoslovak Embassy's commercial section in London is of little use.

In Hungary, Investcenter, and in Poland the Foreign Investment Agency and the Chamber of Commerce are good first stops.

The list of addresses in Chapter 8 provides further details.

INSURANCE

There are two state insurance agencies in Czechoslovakia, the Česká Státní Pojišťovna and the Slovenska Štatna Pojiătovňa.

In Hungary, Investcenter can offer some advice on an increasingly deregulated sector.

The main state enterprise in Poland is Warta Insurance. In July 1990 the government announced it was to base a new legal framework for the insurance industry on the British system.

Export Credit Guarantees Department insurance cover is readily available, but only covers losses of investment incurred as a result of direct appropriation of assets or hostilities. It does not protect against more mundane losses such as fire or theft, nor against losses incurred because of the economic situation.

LANGUAGE AND PRONOUNCIATION

Czechoslovakia

Czech is a Slavonic language, related to Polish and Russian. Out of the population of 15.6 million, 10 million speak Czech, the main language of Bohemia and Moravia. The other national language, Slovakian, can be understood by the Czechs, though often with some superior sniffing. Near the Hungarian frontier, in land which used to belong to Hungary, many still speak Hungarian.

Czech has some sounds which are very difficult for English-speakers to imitate. Some tips for pronunciation may be helpful:

c = *ts* as in fits   ch = *ch* as in loch
č = *ch* as in church   j = *y* as in yes

ř = j as in Jacques   w = v as in van
s = sh as in shy   ž = s as in measure

Hungary

Hungarian is a Finno-Ugric language, related to Finnish and Estonian, and totally unrelated to English, Teutonic, Slav or Romance languages. Although it sounds very attractive, with its lilting intonation, there are no common roots and it is impossible to use guesswork. The spelling is very complex, but with a little effort pronunciation itself is not. Here are some tips:

a = o as in pot   cs = ch as in church
á = a as in rag   j = y as in yes
í = ee as in meet   s = sh as in shop
ó = aw as in tall   sz = s as in sing
c = ts as in fits   zs = s as in measure

Poland

Most people in Poland do not speak English. Other Slav speakers such as Czechs and Slovaks can understand Polish. Pronunciation is horribly difficult. Here are some tips:

ą = aw as in awning   j = y as in yes
c = ts as in fits   ł = w as in wet
ch,h = ch as in loch   ó = oo as in fool
ć,cz = ch as in church   ś,sz = sh as in shop
dż,ż,rz,ź = j as in Jeremy   w = v as in violet
ę = en as in Bengal

Basically, if you meet a word like 'Szczebrzeszynie', call for help!

In terms of foreign languages, the younger generation often know some English, the older ones know German, while the rest proudly talk of the years they spent being forced to learn Russian without being able to speak a word. The best solution, especially during negotiations, is to hire a personal translator/assistant. (See also Translators, page 135.)

LAWYERS

Until the recent reforms in Czechoslovakia, all lawyers were state employees and could be found through the Legal Advice Offices (Advokatni Poradna). Now the sector is increasingly deregulated. The Chamber of Commerce and the local Czechoslovak Embassy can offer a list, but there is enormous competition to acquire the services of the few English-speaking lawyers.

The primary state lawyers' office in Warsaw for foreigners is Zespol Adwokacki No. 40. There is also a Centre of Legal Information and Services, run by the Chamber of Foreign Trade.

The Law Society in Britain set up a committee on Eastern Europe in January 1988, and has information on lawyers specialising in the area. Various associations such as the British-Czechoslovak Law Association, the British-Hungarian Law Association and the British-Polish Legal Association have been established.

MARKET RESEARCH

The Czechoslovak Chamber of Commerce can carry out studies into particular areas, or collate information on specific enterprises for Western firms.

In Hungary, market surveys can be commissioned from the Institute for Economic and Market Research, or from its business subsidiary, Kopconsult. Another useful source is the National Institute for Market Research.

In 1978, Poland established an independent market research institute. It is run on a profit-making basis and can be a useful supplement to a company's own research.

The Association of British Chambers of Commerce runs an Export Market Research Scheme, and government grants may be available to speed up the process.

NATIONAL HOLIDAYS

Czechoslovakia
January 1, Easter Monday, May 1, May 9, October 28, December 25, December 26.

Hungary
January 1, March 15, April 4, Easter Monday, May 1, August 20, December 25, December 26.

Poland
January 1, Easter Monday, Corpus Christi (9th Thursday after Easter), May 1, May 3, June 14, July 22, August 15, November 1 (All Saints), November 11, December 25, December 26.

OFFICE HOURS

Czechoslovakia
Offices: Mon-Fri 0830–1715

Banks: Mon-Fri 0800–1400
Shops: Mon-Sat 0830–1200 and 1400–1800. In the centre of
Prague shops often do not close for lunch.

Hungary
Offices: Mon-Fri 0800–1630
Banks: Mon-Fri 0900–1300 and Sat 0900–1100
Shops: Mon-Sat 0830–1800

Poland
Offices: Mon-Fri 0800–1500 or 0900–1600
Banks: Mon-Fri 0900–1200
Shops: Mon-Sat 0600 or 0700–1800 or 1900

OFFICE SPACE
Until the reforms occurred, only the Czechoslovak Federal Ministry of Foreign Trade (Department 6) had jurisdiction over which
companies could establish offices in Czechoslovakia. Office space
itself was organised through the diplomatic services section of the
Ministry of Foreign Trade. These controls have now disappeared,
and foreign rental agencies are moving in.

A law passed in July 1990 simplified the procedures involved
in setting up a commercial representation. Firms must register,
usually with the Federal Ministry of Foreign Trade. Their docu-
ments should be processed within the month, and they then have
only thirty days within which to sort out office space. Rents
fluctuate, but basically they are high and the law of the souk
prevails. Given the thirty-day rule, firms should have their eye on
a property before they apply for registration. Owners can negotiate
directly, and outside central Prague are limited to a fixed sum
established by decree.

In Budapest finding office space is a nightmare. For fifteen years
no one was allowed to build new office buildings since they were
classified as non-productive. For political reasons, the government
cannot now release space for offices because there is also a housing
shortage. A foreign company must announce its intention of
opening an office to the Ministry of Trade, along with a 20,000
forint ($300) fee, and documents testifying to the company's good
faith. So-called 'technical information offices' – officially restricted
to merely providing advice – do not pay tax, while 'commercial
offices' – entitled to sign contracts and so forth – do. The company
can then, in theory (and for a price), hand over all the practical
details (finding offices, telephone lines, staff, and so on) to PK

(Pénzintézeti Központ, Central Corporation of Banking Companies). Once the Ministry of Trade has approved the office, the company can then register with the Court of Registration for 3,000 forints ($45), and meanwhile it can already begin trading.

Rents can be anything from $5 to $40 per square metre, and companies may have to budget for extra expenditure in the way of bribes to obtain extra telephone lines. Prices of $2,000 per foreman per telephone line are not unknown. Alternatively, a four-month wait might be an optimistic estimate.

In Poland, too, there is a distinction between commercial offices and technical information offices. The latter do not pay tax but are restricted in their economic activities. Permission to open an office must be sought through the Ministry of Foreign Trade's legal department. Telephones are installed by the municipal government authority for each area; telex machines by the telecommunications centre. The Marriott Hotel and Intraco rent rooms to serve as offices, but are booked up years in advance.

In 1990 rents rose rapidly with inflation but were still very low. A monthly rent of 5,000 zloty ($0.5) per square metre for central Warsaw in January had reached only 30,000 zloty ($3.10) by June.

PERMIT REQUIREMENTS
The entry visa requirements for British nationals entering Czechoslovakia and Hungary were abandoned in 1990, though residence and labour permits are required. These can be obtained from the Ministry of Home Affairs.

A visa is still necessary for Poland, available for £20 from the Polish Embassy with a few days notice.

POST
Post is not too bad from Czechoslovakia or Hungary, but it can take two or three weeks for a letter to get from Poland to Britain. Telexes should be used whenever possible.

PROPERTY
In Czechoslovakia outright purchase of property is not permitted by foreigners.

In Hungary foreign private individuals can buy property only if certain strict conditions are met. These include possessing a permanent residence, identity card, or exchanging property already owned. Requests are monitored by the Central Corporation of Banking Companies. Foreign economic associations run with foreign participation, such as joint ventures, can purchase such property as is deemed necessary to carry out their business. This is broadly interpreted to include, for instance, accommodation for employees. Wholly foreign-owned companies still have to prove that they need the property for their economic activity. A list of properties availiable is kept at a local real estate register and can be consulted by the public.

In Poland, companies established by foreign parties can purchase or lease privately owned land. If the foreign party owns 50% or more of the company, the Ministry of Internal Affairs must give permission. State-owned property may be leased to companies for perpetual use, but not sold.

SECURITY CONTROLS

Although CoCom regulations have eased, it is worth checking that there are no restrictions on technological or chemical goods. The CoCom section at the DTI provides a list of goods.

TELEPHONE CODES

Czechoslovakia
International operator: 0132
Directory enquiries in Prague: 120
Directory enquiries elsewhere: 121
Dialling Britain: 00 44

Hungary
International operator: 1186 977
English-speaking operator: 1172 200
Dialling Britain: 00 44
To dial directly from Budapest to other towns in Hungary, dial 06, wait for a tone, and then add the area code and local number.

Poland
International operator: 901/902/903/904
Dialling Britain: 00 [wait for an extra dialling tone] 44

TIME
Eastern Europe observes Standard European Time, GMT +1 hour, and Summer Time, GMT +2 hours.

TIPPING
Ten per cent is usual for waiters, taxis, petrol stations and hairdressers, with small sums for hotel staff. Hard-currency tips are particularly appreciated.

TRADE FAIRS

The largest Czech exhibition is the Brno International Engineering Fair, held in September, which in 1990 attracted exhibitors from thirty-three countries, including sixty from Britain. Contracts worth 7.5 billion crowns ($330 million) were concluded, 75% of which were with partners from market economy countries[5]. The equivalent Hungarian exhibition is the Budapest International Fair, held twice a year, in May for investment goods, and in autumn for consumer goods. The main Polish exhibition is the Poznań International Trade Fair held in June, which covers all trade sectors. There are also specialised mining, medical, agricultural, book and computer fairs.

TRADE UNIONS

The newly formed Czechoslovak Confederation of Trade Unions, with six million members, is likely to favour economic policies which defend workers' jobs.

Hungary's old official trade unions face diminishing membership as unemployment begins to grow. Agreements such as that at Ganz-Hunslet locomotive works, whereby the former national union is banned in favour of a small works' syndicate, have become common. In theory, worker participation in management is mandatory in joint ventures with more than 200 employees, and one third of the Supervisory Board must be workers. However the Supervisory Boards' influence is declining rapidly.

Poland, of course, is a special case, given the trade union movement and Solidarity's pre-eminent role in politics. It is likely to be torn between its eagerness for free market reform and its desire to safeguard workers' interests.

TRANSLATORS

Companies keen to do business with the West will usually supply an interpreter. It is, however, a very good idea to bring your own, who has your interests at heart. There are many freelance translators and interpreters trying their chances, and recommendations are often word-of-mouth. German can be useful with the older generation, though sometimes unpopular in Poland. English is not yet commonly spoken.

In Czechoslovakia official help is available through the Prague Information Service.

In Hungary, the State Translation Bureau can provide official translations, and in Poland translators can be hired through NOT, particularly if technical interpreters are required.

TRANSPORT

The domestic air network within Czechoslovakia provides regular daily flights to most provincial towns. There is a Cedok bus from Prague airport to the main hotels.During the major trade fairs there is an express bus link between Vienna and Brno. A rapid hydrofoil links Vienna with Bratislava during its trade fair.

The metro, tram and bus services in Prague are efficient. The same ticket is valid on all three, but must be bought in advance at the metro stations, tobacconists or shops displaying the notice 'Predprodej Jizdenek'. Tickets are punched in a time-stamping machine at the entrance to the trams or metro stations, and entitle passengers to ninety minutes of unlimited travel. Since the revolution street names, and some metro names, have been changed, usually from a Communist leader to a more fashionable hero. Thus Lenin station has become Dejvicka, and Gottwaldova is now Vysehrad. A recent map is essential. Taxis have been deregulated, and drivers are now asking inflated rates.

Budapest is only three and a half hours by train from Vienna, four hours by car or five hours by hydrofoil, booked through IBUSZ. Trains from Vienna arrive at Keleti Pü (East station). There is an airport bus service from Ferihegy airport at thirty-minute intervals. The journey to the city centre takes around forty minutes. For city buses, tickets must be bought before boarding at 'Trafik' tobacconists or main shops, and validated in a ticket-punch. Each ticket is valid for one journey by tram, bus or metro. Buses with red route numbers are express buses and do not stop everywhere. Red-route buses labelled 'E' can provide an unpleasant shock as they travel non-stop between the two termini of the route, and tough luck if you want to get off in between. Taxis from international hotel ranks often charge exhorbitant fees, and since they have been deregulated, Budapest cab drivers are becoming notorious at overcharging Westerners. Traffic jams are now frequent in Budapest.

In Warsaw tickets for trams and buses must be bought before travelling at 'Ruch' booths. Express buses require two tickets. Taxis are easy to find because most Poles can no longer afford to use them. Fares on the taxi meter may have to be multiplied by a certain official factor to arrive at the correct price. The roads are not yet overcrowded in Warsaw. The airport is only 7 km from the city, and there are good links between the two.

CHAPTER 8

ADDRESSES

GENERAL

Association of British Chambers
of Commerce
4 Westwood House
Westwood Business Park
Coventry CV4 8HS
Tel: 0203 694484
Fax: 0203 694690

Birmingham Chamber
of Commerce
PO Box 360
75 Harborne Road
Birmingham B15 3DH
Tel: 021 454 6171
Fax: 021 455 8670

British International
Freight Association
Redfern House
Browells Lane
Feltham
Middlesex TW13 7EP
Tel: 081 844 2266
Fax: 081 890 5546

CoCom
Export Control Organisation
Department of Trade and
Industry
Kingsgate House
Victoria Street
London SW1E 6SW
Tel: 071 215 8032/3
Fax: 071 215 8564/8202

Commission of the European
Communities
Rue de la loi 200
B-1049 Brussels
Tel: 010 322 235 1111
Tlx: 21877 COMEU B

> Pierre Mirel
> Industrial Restructuring
> Initiatives

> Gwenole Cozigou
> External Relations
> (Vocational training)
> DG I

> Thérèse Sobieski
> External Relations
> (Environmental Protection)
> DG I

> John Maddison
> Agriculture
> DG VI

or in London

Jean Monnet House
8 Storey's Gate
London SW1P 3AT
Tel: 071 222 8122/8109

Confederation of British Industry
Centre Point
103 New Oxford Street
London WC1A 1DU
Tel: 071 379 7400
Fax: 071 497 2597

East European Trade Council
Suite 10
Westminster Palace Gardens
Artillery Row
London SW1P 1RL
Tel: 071 222 7622
Fax: 071 222 5359

European Bank for
Reconstruction & Development
(EBRD or BERD)
6 Broadgate
Level 7
London EC2M 2QS
Tel: 071 496 0060
Fax: 071 628 6088

European Investment Bank
100 Boulevard Konrad Adenauer
62950 Luxembourg
Tel: 010 352 43790
Fax: 010 352 437704
Tlx: 3530 bnkeu ln

or

European Investment Bank
68 Pall Mall
London SW1Y 5ES
Tel: 071 839 3351
Fax: 071 930 9929
Tlx: 919 159

Export Credits Guarantee
Department
Export House
50 Ludgate Hill
London EC4M 2AY
Tel: 071 382 7542
Tlx: 883601 a/b ECGDHQ
(A-C) LDN
Fax: 071 382 7649

Export Intelligence Service
Lime Grove
Eastcote
Middlesex HA4 8RS
Tel: 081 866 8771
Fax: 081 866 9535

Export Market Information
Centre
1–19 Victoria Street
London SW1H 0ET
Tel: 071 215 5444/5445
Tlx: 8811074/5 DTHQ G
Fax: 071 215 4231

Export Opportunities Ltd
Export House
87A Wembley Hill Road
Wembley
Middlesex HA9 8BU
Tel: 081 900 1313
Fax: 081 900 1268

The Great Britain/East
Europe Centre
31 Knightsbridge
London SW1X 7NH
Tel: 071 245 9771

HOTS Training
PEP3D/DTI
Room 225
1 Victoria Street
London SW1H 0ET
Tel: 071 215 4945
Fax: 071 222 2531

Industrial Co-operation and
Funds Mobilisation Division
United Nations Industrial
Development Organisation
Vienna International Centre
PO Box 300
A-1400 Vienna
Austria
Tel: 010 431 211 310
Tlx: 135 612 uno a
Fax: 010 431 232 156

International Finance
Corporation
New Zealand House
Haymarket
London SW1Y 4TE
Tel: 071 930 8741
Fax: 071 321 0589

International Monetary Fund
700 19th Street NW
Washington DC
20431 USA
Tel: 010 1202 623 7430
Fax: 202 623 7201

Know-How Fund
Joint Assistance Unit
Eastern European Department
Foreign and Commonwealth
Office
King Charles Street
London SW1A 2AH
Tel: 071 270 2944 (General)
    071 270 3469 (Poland,
    Czechoslovakia & Hungary)
Fax: 071 270 3012

Law Society
Legal Practice (International)
50 Chancery Lane
London WC2A 1SX
Tel: 071 242 1222
Fax: 071 831 0057

London Chamber of Commerce
(East European Section)
69 Cannon Street
London EC4N 5AB
Tel: 071 248 4444
Fax: 071 489 0391

Ministry of Agriculture (MAFF)
Whitehall Place (East Bloc)
London SW1A 2HH
Tel: 071 270 8148
Fax: 071 270 8276

Overseas Development Agency
Recruitment and Consultancies
Abercrombie House
Easglesham Road
East Kilbride
Glasgow G75 8EA
Tel: 03552 41199
Fax: 03552 38432

Overseas Project Fund
PEP5D/DTI
Room 206
1 Victoria Street
London SW1H 0ET
Tel: 071 215 4834
Fax: 071 222 2629

Simpler Trade Procedures Board
Venture House
29 Glasshouse Street
London W1R 5RG
Tel: 071 287 3525
Fax: 071 287 5751

Technical Help to the Exporter
British Standards Institute
Linford Wood
Milton Keynes MK14 6LE
Tel: 0908 220 022

World Aid Section
Department of Trade and
Industry
Room 036
1 Victoria Street
London SW1H 0ET
Tel: 071 215 4255
Fax: 071 222 2629

CZECHOSLOVAKIA

IN BRITAIN

British–Czechoslovak Law Assoc.
c/o Centre for Commercial
Law Studies
Queen Mary & Westfield College
339 Mile End Road
London E1 4NS
Tel: 071 975 5127

Brno International
Engineering Fair
c/o John Haigh Services
14 Station Way
Peckham
London SE15 4RX
Tel: 071 639 7265

Tlx: 928699 haigex g
Fax: 071 358 0966

CSA (Czechoslovak Airlines)
12a Margaret Street
London W1
Tel: 071 255 1898

Cedok (Czechoslovak
Tourist Agency)
17–18 Old Bond Street
London W1X 4RB
Tel: 071 629 6058
Fax: 071 493 7841

Czechoslovak Embassy
25–26 Kensington Palace Gardens
London W8
Tel: 071 229 1255
Fax: 071 727 9654

Overseas Trade Division 3/5 OTD
Czechoslovakia Section
Department of Trade and Industry
1 Victoria Street
London SW1H 0ET
Tel: 071 215 5152/5267
Tlx: 8811074 a/b DTHQ G
Fax: 071 215 5269

Merchants Bank
104/106 Leadenhall Street
London EC3A 4AA
Tel: 071 623 3201
Tlx: 885 069
Fax: 071 283 5372

Vitrea (Merchants) Ltd
(Countertrade Organisation)
12 Clerkenwell Rd
London EC1M 5PP
Tel: 071 253 1625
Fax: 071 490 0088
Tlx: 288 67

IN CZECHOSLOVAKIA

Advokatni Poradna 1
(Legal Offices)
Národní Třída 32
CS 116 66 Prague 1

Tel: 010 422 224 782/236 8150
Tlx: 122 991 app c

First Secretary (Commercial)
British Embassy
Blanická 13 (3rd floor)
120 00 Prague 2
Tel: 010 422 258 685
Tlx: 122926/252907
Fax: 010 422 250 986

BVV/Brno Fairs and Exhibitions
Brno International
Engineering Fair
Brno House of Technology
Czechoslovak Scientific–
Technical Society
Výstaviště 1
CS 602 00
Brno
Tel: 010 425 314 1111
Tlx: 622 39

Cedok Travel Agents
Na Přikopé 18
111 35 Prague 1
Tel: 010 422 212 7111
Tlx: 121109
Fax: 010 422 232 1981

Chamber of Commerce of
Czechoslovakia
Argentinská 38
170 05 Prague 7
Tel: 010 422 875 368/872
4867/875 461
Tlx: 121 862 obko
Fax: 010 422 879 134

Chamber of Commerce of
Czechoslovakia
Gorkého nám. 9
816 03 Bratislava
Tel: 010 427 54596
Tlx: 92586 obkom c

CS Trading Co. Ltd
(Counter-trade Organisation)
Kodanska 46
CS 100 10 Praha 10

Tel: 010 422 749 075
Tlx: 122 134
Fax: 010 422 737 422

CTK – Made-In ... (Publicity)
Advertising Agency
Kotorska 16
CS 140 04 Prague 4
Tel: 010 422 422 1558/
420 1589/422 151
Tlx: 122501 mip c

CTK (Brno Office)
Solnicni 5
CS 657 25
Brno
Tel: 010 425 221 88
Tlx: 624 29 ctkbo c

CTK (Bratislava Office)
Jiraskova 5
Bratislava
Tel: 010 427 331 115

Czech Entrepreneurs Association
(Sdružení Československých
Podnikatelů)
Staroměstské nám 6
110 00 Prague 1
Tel: 010 422 232 0752

Czechoslovak Scientific Technical
Society
(Ceskoslovenska
vedeckotechnicka spolecnost,
CSVTS)
Siroka 5
110 00 Prague 1
Tel: 010 422 232 1251

Federal Statistical Office
(Federalni statisticky urad)
Sokolovska 142
Prague 8 – Karlin

Foreign Insurance Department
(Management for Foreign Affairs)
Spálená 16
Prague 1
Tel: 010 422 214 8111

Incheba (Trade Fair)
2 Makarenkova
CS 852 51
Bratislava
Tel: 010 427 801 1111
Tlx: 922 55 inche c
Fax: 010 427 846 736

Ministry of Finance
(Foreign Exchange Section)
Ministerstvo Financi
Letenská 15
110 00 Prague 1
Tel: 010 422 514 1111
Tlx: 121 868
Fax: 010 422 534 498/535 759

Ministry of Foreign Trade
(Federalni ministerstvo
zahranicniho obchodu)
Politických vězňů 20
122 49 Prague 1
Tel: 010 422 126 1111
Tlx: 121 808/121 077
Fax: 010 422 322 868/322 861

PIS (Prague Information Service)
Translating and Interpreting
Services
Za Poříčskou bránou 7
180 00 Prague 8
Tel: 010 422 236 7131/2

Rapid
(Foreign Trade Publicity
Organisation)
ul. 28 Rijna 13
112 79 Prague 1
Tel: 010 422 213 911
Tlx: 121 142 reag c
Fax: 010 422 232 7520

Transakta
(Counter-trade Organisation)
Letenská 11
118 19 Prague 1
Tel: 010 422 514 1111/539 211
Tlx: 934 66

Union of Production
Co-operatives
(Svaz vyrobnich druzstev)
Jindrisska 2
110 00 Prague 1
Tel: 010 422 265 271

USOZ
Association of Czechoslovak
Foreign Trade Agencies
Na strzi 63 (Motokov Building)
140 62 Prague 4
Tel: 010 422 414 1111
Tlx: 121 355
Fax: 010 422 434 690

BANKS
Czechoslovak Commercial Bank
(Ceskoslovenska Obchodni banka)
Na Přikopé 14
115 20 Prague 1
Tel: 010 422 2132, 220 541
Tlx: 122 201
Fax: 010 422 232 7562

General Credit Bank
(Vseobecna uverova banka)
Leningradska 20
818 54 Bratislava
Tel: 010 427 319 1111
Tlx: 93346–7

Girozentrale (Austrian)
Václavské nám. 41
112 83 Prague 1
Tel: 010 422 267 588

Investment Bank
(Investicni banka)
Na Přikopé 28
110 00 Prague 1
Tel: 010 422 2112
Tlx: 122 682
Fax: 010 422 235 4141

Merchant's Bank
(Živnostenská banka)
Na Přikopé 20
Nové Město

110 00 Prague 1
Tel: 010 422 224 346
Tlx: 122 313
Fax: 010 422 263 381

Société Générale (French)
Vodičkova 34
110 10 Prague 1
Tel: 010 422 241 690
Tlx: 123 356

State Bank of Czechoslovakia
(Statni Banka Ceskoslovenska)
Na Přikopé 28
110 03 Prague 1
Tel: 010 422 236 4621
Tlx: 121 831, 122 628
Fax: 010 422 235 4141

HOTELS
Alcron
Štěpánská 40,
Nové Město
110 00 Prague 1
Tel: 010 422 235 9216
Tlx: 121 814

Europa
Václavské nám. 29,
Nové Město
110 00 Prague 1
Tel: 010 422 263 905

Forum
Kongresova Ulice
140 69 Prague 4
Tel: 010 422 410 111
Tlx: 122 100 ihfp c
Fax: 010 422 420 684

Inter-Continental
Náměsti Curieovych 43/5,
Staré Město
110 00 Prague 1
Tel: 010 422 231 1812
Tlx: 122 681
Fax: 010 422 231 0500

Interhotel Panorama Praha
Milevska 7
140 63 Prague 4
Tel: 010 422 416 1111
Tlx: 123 576
Jalta
Václavské nám. 45,
Nové Město
110 00 Prague 1
Tel: 010 422 265 541
Tlx: 121 580

3 Ostrichs Hotel
Dračickeho nám. 12
Mala Strana
Prague 1
Tel: 010 422 536 151

Parkhotel
Veletrzni 20
170 00 Prague 7
Tel: 010 422 380 7111
Tlx: 122 278

Splendid
Ovenacka 33
170 00 Prague 7
Tel: 010 422 373 351

Interhotel Devin Hotel
Riecna
897 21 Bratislava
Tel: 010 427 308 51
Tlx: 934 82

Hotel International
Husova 16
656 67 Brno
Tel: 010 425 264 11
Tlx: 622 47/9

CAR HIRE
Pragocar
Štěpánská 42
Prague 1
Tel: 010 422 235 2825 or 235 2809
Tlx: 122 729

Pragocar
Airport Rental
Tel: 010 422 367 807

Pragocar
Intercontinental Hotel
Tel: 010 422 231 9595

Avis
Prague Airport
Tel: 010 422 334 4370

Avis
Štěpánská
Prague
Tel: 010 422 267 417
Tlx: 123 155

Hertz
Palace Hotel
Prague
Tel: 010 422 236 1637

Pragocar Bratislava
Hviezdoslavovo nám. 14
Bratislava
Tel: 010 427 333 233

Brnocar
Solnicni
Brno
Tel: 010 425 240 39

HUNGARY

IN BRITAIN
Overseas Trade Division
3/5 (OTD)
Hungarian Section
Department of Trade and Industry
1 Victoria Street
London SW1H 0ET
Tel: 071 215 4734/5257
Tlx: 881 1074 a/b DTHQ G
Fax: 071 222 2629

Danube Travel Limited
6 Conduit Street
London W1R 9TG
Tel: 071 493 0263
Tlx: 23541

Hungarian Embassy
Commercial Secretary
46 Eaton Place
London SW1

Tel: 071 235 8767/9 or 235 7680
Tlx: 28874

Hungarian International Bank Ltd
Prince's House
95 Gresham Street
London EC2V 7LU
Tel: 071 606 5371
Fax: 071 606 8565
Tlx: 887 206

ITF International Agencies Ltd
Representative   for   Hungarian
Fairs
Radcliffe House
Blenheim Court
West Midlands
Solihull B91 3BG
Tel: 021 705 6707
Tlx: 337 073

Malév Hungarian Airlines
10 Vigo Street
London W1X 1AJ
Tel: 071 439 0577
Tlx: 24841
Fax: 071 734 8116

IN HUNGARY
Academy of Sciences
Roosevelt tér 9
H-1051 Budapest
Tel: 010 361 111 3400/138 2344
Tlx: 224 139 mtaka h

British Airways
Apáczai Csere János utca 5
1052 Budapest
Tel: 010 361 118 3299/118 3041

First Secretary (Commercial)
British Embassy
Harmincad utca 6
1051 Budapest V
Tel: 010 361 118 2888/117 1430
Tlx: 224527 a/b BRIT H

Chamber of Commerce
(Magyar Gazdasagi Kamara)
Kossuth Lájos tér 6–8

1055 Budapest
H-1389 POB 106
Tel: 010 361 153 3333
Tlx: 224745 MGK H
Fax: 010 361 153 1285

Danubia Patent Bureau
Bajcsy-Zsilinszky út 16
Budapest V
H-1368, POB 198
Tel: 010 361 118 1111
Tlx: 225 872

Hungarocoop
(Hungarian Cooperative Foreign
Trading Co.)
Október 6 utca 12
H 1370 Budapest
Tel: 010 361 153 1711
Tlx: 224 859

Hungexpo
The Hungarian Foreign Trade
Office for Fairs & Publicity
Division of Budapest International
Fairs & Exhibitions
Dobi István út 10
H-1441 Budapest
POB 44
Tel: 010 361 157 3555
Tlx: 224 188

Hungexpo Advertising Agency
Varosliget
H-1441 Budapest
POB 44
Tel: 010 361 122 5008
Tlx: 224 525
Fax: 010 361 122 1021

Ibusz – Hungarian Travel Agency
Tanacs körut 3/c
Budapest VII
Tel: 010 361 142 3140
Tlx: 225 650
or

Ibusz
Felszabadulás tér 5
1364 Budapest

Tel: 010 361 118 0421
Tlx: 22 5941
Fax: 010 361 1177 723

Inland Revenue Office
(Adó-és Pénzügyi Ellenôrzési
Hivatal)
Széchenyi u. 2
1054 Budapest
Tel: 010 361 118 1896
Tlx: 223 254 apeh h

Institute for Economic and
Market Research
Dorottya u. 6
H 1389 Budapest V
Tel: 010 361 118 4055
Tlx: 225 646

Intercooperation Co Ltd
Attila ut 14
Budapest 1
POB 53
Tel: 010 361 115 2220
Tlx: 224 242

International Trade Centre
Váci utca 19–21
H 1052 Budapest
Tel: 010 361 118 8749
Tlx: 227 704

Interpress
Publicity, Publishing and
Printing House
Mihály E.u. 14
H 1022 Budapest
Tel: 010 361 135 0945
Tlx: 226 506

Investcenter
Office for Foreign
Investment Promotion
Dorottya u. 4
1389 Budapest
Tel: 010 361 118 6064
Tlx: 225 191
Fax: 010 361 118 3732

Mahir
Hungarian Publicity Company
POB 367
H 1053 Budapest
Tel: 010 361 118 3444
Tlx: 225 341
Fax: 010 361 117 9032

Malév
Váci utca 1–3
H1052 Budapest
Tel: 010 361 118 4333
Tlx: 225 794

Ministry of Finance
(Pènzügyminisztèrium)
József nádor tér 2–4
1051 Budapest
Tel: 010 361 118 5670
Tlx: 225 942
Fax: 010 361 118 2570

Ministry of Foreign Affairs
(Külügyminisztèrium)
Bem rakpart 47
H1394 Budapest II
Tel: 010 361 156 8000/135 0100
Tlx: 225 571

Ministry of Industry
Ipari
Martirok utca 85
H 1024 Budapest
Tel: 010 361 156 5566
Tlx: 225 376 ipmin h
Fax: 010 361 155 3482

Ministry of Trade
(Kereskedelmi Miniszterium)
Honvéd utca 13–15
H-1880 Budapest V
Tel: 010 361 153 0000
Tlx: 225 578 kkm h
Fax: 010 361 153 2794

National Institute for
Market Research
Szende Pál utca 3
H 1373 Budapest

Tel: 010 361 118 5044/5225
Tlx: 225 064

OMKDK-Technoinform
(Foreign Trade Division of the
Hungarian Central Technical
Library & Documentation
Centre)
Múzeum 17
Budapest VIII
Tel: 010 361 133 6309
Tlx: 224 944

Post Office
Váci utca 34
H 1052 Budapest

PK (See Banks: Central
Corporation of Banking
Companies)

State Assets Management Agency
(Allami Vagyonügynökség)
Szent István tér 11
1055 Budapest V
Tel: 010 361 132 9360
Tlx: 226 941

State Translation Bureau
Bajza utca 52
Budapest VI
Tel: 010 361 112 9610

State Wage and Labour Office
(Allami Bér és Munkaügi
Hivatal)
Roosevelt tér 7–8
1051 Budapest
Tel: 010 361 132 2100

Central Statistical Office
Kozponti Statiszikai Hivatal
Keleti Karoly utca 5–7
1024 Budapest
Tel: 010 361 115 2850
Tlx: 224 308 stati h

Stock Exchange
Tel: 010 361 117 5226

Tax and Financial Supervisory
Office
Ado es Penzügyi Ellenörzesi
Hivatal
Szechenyi utca 2
H 1054 Budapest
Tel: 010 361 112 1890
Tlx: 223 254 apeh h

Taxis, Budapest: Fötaxi: 122 1222
Volántaxi: 166 6666

BANKS
Agrobank
Széchenyi rakpart 6
H 1054 Budapest
Tel: 010 361 111 4732
Tlx: 223 111

Budapest Bank
Deák Ferenc utca 5
H 1052 Budapest
Tel: 010 361 118 1200
Tlx: 223 013
Fax: 010 361 118 2065

Central Bank for Venture
Financing Ltd
(Altalános Vállalkozási Bank Rt)
Stollár Béla utca 3/a
1055 Budapest
Tel: 010 361 132 6590
Tlx: 223 157
Fax: 010 361 131 3181

Central Corporation of
Banking Companies
(Pènzintèzeti Központ)
Szamuely utca 38
1093 Budapest
Tel: 010 361 117 1255
Tlx: 226 548
Fax: 010 361 118 9429

Citibank
Váci utca 19–21
H 1052 Budapest
Tel: 010 361 118 9477
Tlx: 227 822
Fax: 010 361 118 9694

Credit Bank Ltd
(Magyar Hital Bank Rt)
Oktober 6 utca 5
H 1054 Budapest
Tel: 010 361 112 5200

Hungarian Foreign Trade Bank
(see State Assets Management
Agency)

Inter-Europa Bank Ltd
H 1054 Budapest
Szabadság tér 15
Tel: 010 361 132 0170
Fax: 010 361 153 4850
Tlx: 22 7878 inves h

National Bank of Hungary
(Magyar Nemzeti Bank)
Szabadság tér 8–9
H 1850 Budapest
Tel: 010 361 153 3044
Tlx: 227 267
Fax: 010 361 153 1058

National Savings Bank
(Országos Takarékpénztár)
Münnich Ferenc utca 16
H 1051 Budapest
Tel: 010 361 117 2106
Tlx: 227 540

PRESS
Business Partner Hungary
Dorottya utca 6
H 1389 Budapest V
Tel: 010 361 117 0850
Tlx: 22 5646
Fax: 010 361 118 3732

Hungarian Book Agency
87 Sewardstone Road
London E2 9HN
Tel: 081 980 9096

Hungarian Business Herald
Hungaropress Economic
Information
Hungarian Digest
All from: Kultura

H 1389 Budapest 62
POB 149

The Hungarian Observer
Budapest XIV
Lumumba utca 207
H 1145
Tel: 010 361 251 4296
Tlx: 226 578 sptex h

Hungarian Trade Journal
Lenin körút 9–11
H 1073 Budapest

Invest in Hungary
Interpress Expo Budapest
Bockskai út 21
H 1114 Budapest
Tel: 010 361 186 9420
Tlx: 226 506

Made In Hungary
MTI
H 1426 Budapest
POB 3
Tel: 010 361 175 6722
Tlx: 224 371

HOTELS
Hungarohotels Reservations and
Tourist Services
Petöfi Sándor utca 16
H 1502 Budapest V
Tel: 010 361 118 3393
Tlx: 224 923

Atrium Hyatt
Roosevelt tér 2
H 1051 Budapest
Tel: 010 361 138 3000
Tlx: 225 485

Buda Penta
Krisztina körút 41–43
H 1013 Budapest
Tel: 010 361 156 6333
Tlx: 225 495

Forum
Apáczai Csere János utca 12–14
H 1052 Budapest

Tel: 010 361 117 8088
Tlx: 224 178
Fax: 010 361 117 9808

Gellért
Szent Gellért tér 1
H 1111 Budapest
Tel: 010 361 185 2200
Tlx: 224 363

Hilton
Hess András tér 1–3
H 1014 Budapest
Tel: 010 361 171 5000
Tlx: 225 984

Novotel
Alkotás utca 63–67
H 1444 Budapest
Tel: 010 361 186 9588
Tlx: 225 496

Palace
Rákóczi ut 43
H 1088 Budapest
Tel: 010 361 113 6000
Tlx: 224 217

Royal
Lenin körút 47–49
1073 Budapest VII
Tel: 010 361 153 3133

Arany Bika
4025 Vörös Hadsereg utca 11–15
Debrecen
Tel: 010 3652 16777

Pannónia
7621 Rákóczi utca 3
Pécs
Tel: 010 3672 13322

CAR HIRE
Budget
Ferihegy Airport
Budapest
Tel: 010 361 134 2540

Fötaxi
VIII Kertész utca 24–28
H 1073 Budapest

Tel: 010 361 122 1471
Tlx: 226 222

Fötaxi-Hertz
Aranykéz utca 4–8
Budapest
Tel: 010 361 117 7533
Tlx: 223 252

Ibusz-Avis
Martinelli tér 8
Budapest
Tel: 010 361 118 4158
Tlx: 225 545
Fax: 010 361 118 4859

Volantourist-Europcar
Vaskapu utca 16
Budapest
Tel: 010 361 133 4783
Tlx: 225 639

POLAND

IN BRITAIN

Anglo-DAL Ltd
(Countertrade Organisation)
Anglo-Dal House
5 Spring Villa Road
Edgware
Middlesex HA8 7EB
Tel: 081 951 5050
Tlx: 238 25/6
Fax: 081 951 4814

LOT Polish Airlines
313 Regent Street
London W1
Tel: 071 580 5037

Overseas Trade Division
Polish Section
Department of Trade
and Industry
1 Victoria Street
London SW1H 0ET
Tel: 071 215 4734/5

Tlx: 8811074 a/b DTHQ G
Fax: 071 215 4743

Polish Cultural Institute
34 Portland Place
London W1N 4HQ
Tel: 071 636 6032/3

Polish Embassy
Commercial Section
15 Devonshire Street
London W1N 2AR
Tel: 071 580 5481
Tlx: 28193
Fax: 071 323 0195

Polish Travel Agency
(Tazab Travel Ltd)
273 Old Brompton Road
London SW5 9JB
Tel: 071 373 1186
Tlx: 919576

Polorbis Travel Ltd
82 Mortimer Street
Regent Street
London W1N 7DE
Tel: 071 637 4971
Tlx: 8812232
Fax: 071 436 6558

United Baltic Corporation
Dexter House
2 Royal Mint Court
London EC3 N4XX
Tel: 071 265 0808
Tlx: 887392
Fax: 071 481 4784

IN POLAND

AGPOL Advertising Agency
ul. Kierbedzia 4
00 957 Warsaw
POB 7
Tel: 010 4822 269 221
Tlx: 813 567

British Airways Airport Office
Tel: 010 4822 460 572
Tlx: 813 405

British Airways Booking Office
Krucza 49
00 120 Warsaw
Tel: 010 4822 289 431/2

British Council
Aleje Jerozolimskie 59
00 697 Warsaw
Tel: 010 4822 287 401/3
Tlx: 812555 BRIN PL

British Consulate
ul. Wawelska 14
Tel: 010 4822 258 031
Fax: 010 4822 250 328

First Secretary (Commercial)
British Embassy
Aleja Róz 1
00 556 Warsaw
Tel: 010 48 22 281 001/2/3/4/5
Tlx: 813694 PROD PL
Fax: 010 4822 217 161

Central Customs Office
ul. Świętokrzyska 12
00 950 Warsaw
Tel: 010 4822 200 311
Tlx: 814 427

Central Railway Station (PKS)
Warszawa Centralna
Al. Jerozolimskie 54
Tel: 010 4822 255 000
 Local train connections
 information:
 010 4822 200 361
 International connections:
 010 4822 204 512/257 554

Central Statistical Office
Al. Niepodległości 208
00 925 Warsaw
Tel: 010 4822 253 241

Central Tourist Information
(COIT)
Pl. Zamkowy 1
Warsaw
Tel: 010 4822 270 000

Centre of Legal Information and
Services
(Centrum Informacji i Uslug
Prawnych)
ul. Trebacka 4
00 950 Warsaw
Tel: 010 4822 260 221

Centrum Badania Rynkow
Market Research Institute
ul. Trebacka 4
POB 362
00 950 Warsaw

Chamber of Foreign Trade
(Polska Izba Handlu
Zagranicznego)
ul. Trebacka 4
POB 361
00 950 Warsaw
Tel: 010 4822 260 221
Tlx: 814361 pihz pl

CINTE
Centrum Informacji Naukowej,
Technicznej i Ekonomicznej
(Centre of Scientific, Technical &
Economic Information)
Al. Niedpodleglości 186
POB 355
00 950 Warsaw
Tel: 010 4822 251 241
Tlx: 813716

DAL International Trading Co.
(Countertrade Organisation)
Ul. Marszalkowska 82
00 517 Warsaw
Tel: 010 4822 280 900
Tlx: 814 831

Dipservice (accommodation)
ul. Swietokrzyska 36–38
00 950 Warsaw

Foreign Investment Agency
Plac Powstańców 1
00 950 Warsaw
Tel: 010 4822 269 041

Tlx: 814291/2/3/4/5 mrw dla
Agencji
Fax: 010 4822 268 593/263
414/261 166

Foreign Investors Chamber of
Industry and Commerce
ul. Krakowskie Przedmieście 47–51
00 325 Warsaw
Tel: 010 4822 263 201
Tlx: 817 105 inpol pl
Fax: 010 4822 268 593

Fundacja Polska Eksportu
Foundation for Polish Export
ul. Królewska 27
00 060 Warsaw
Tel: 010 4822 276 810

Investment Promotion Service
UNIDO
ul. Stawki 2
00 950 Warsaw
Tel: 010 482 635 7112
Tlx: 817916 unido pl
Fax: 010 4822 635 1260

Intraco (for office
accommodation)
Trade Centre for
Foreign Representation
ul. Stawki 2
00 950 Warsaw
Tlx: 812 341 traco pl

Lawyers Office No. 40
Zespol Adwokacki 40
Hibnera 13
00 012 Warsaw
Tel: 010 4822 274 875

LOT Polish Airlines
17 Stycznia 39
02 148 Warsaw
Tel: 010 4822 461 251
Tlx: 813512

or

ul. Warynskiego 9
Tel: 010 4822 217 021
Tlx: 814 327

Ministry of Finance
Ul. Świętokrzyska 12
00 950 Warsaw
Tel: 010 4822 200 311
Tlx: 815 592 minfin pl

Ministry of Foreign Affairs
Al. 1 Armii Wojska Polskiego 23
00 580 Warsaw
Tel: 010 4822 287 451
Tlx: 814301 msz pl

Ministry of Foreign Economic
Relations
Plac Trzech Krzyży 5
00 507 Warsaw
Tel: 010 4822 693 500
Tlx: 814501 msz pl
Fax: 010 4822 290 617

Ministry of Foreign Trade
(For Office Permits: Zespol do
Spraw Przedstawicielstwa Firm
Obcych, Legal Department)
ul. Wiejska 10
00 950 Warsaw
Tel: 010 4822 210 331
Tlx: 814 501 mhz pl
Fax: 010 4822 290 617

Ministry of Industry
ul. Wspólna 4
00 505 Warsaw
Tel: 010 4822 282 141
Tlx: 814 267, 814 261

NOT (see Technical Interpreter
Hire)

Office of Employment
(Urzad Zatrudnienia)
ul. Czerniakowska 44
00 717 Warsaw
Tel: 010 4822 412 083/087

Patent Office
Al. Niepodleglości 188/192
00 950 Warsaw
Tel: 010 4822 258 001
Tlx: 813 716 cint pl

Police
Poliga
Tel: 997 (emergency service)

Polservice Foreign Trade
Organisation
Szpitalna 5, POB 335
00 959 Warsaw
Tel: 010 4822 278 061
Tlx: 813 539

Post Office (24 hour: Fax Service)
Warsaw 1 Post Office
Swiętokrzyska 31/33 (Śródmieście)
Tel: 010 4822 266 411
Fax: 010 4822 300 021

Post Office (Telex Service)
Urzad Pocztowy
ul. Nowogrodzka 45
02 002 Warsaw

Poznań International Trade Fair
ul. Głogowska 14
60 734 Poznań
Tel: 010 4861 692 592
Tlx: 413251 targ pl
Fax: 010 4861 665 827

Solidarity Economic Foundation
NSZZ Solidarnosc
Waly Piastowskie 24
80855 Gdansk

Stowarzyszenie Marketingu
(Association of Marketing)
Nowy Swiat 49
00 042 Warsaw
Tel: 010 4822 276 239

Technical Interpreter Hire
NOT Naczelnia Organizacja
Techniczna
Czackiego 3/5
00 043 Warsaw
Tel: 010 4822 273 610
Tlx: 813225

Torimex Foreign Trade
Organisation
Office I
Nowogrodzka 35/41, POB 394
00 950 Warsaw
Tel: 010 4822 296 011
Tlx: 813611

US Trade Development Centre
ul. Wiejska 20
00 490 Warsaw
Tel: 010 4822 214 515
Tlx: 813934

Warsaw Centre for Technical
Progress (OPT)
(Osrodek Postepu Technicznego)
Palac Kultury i Nauki, Ground
Floor
00 901 Warsaw
Tel: 010 4822 200 211
Tlx: 814469

Warsaw International Airport
Tel: 010 4822 469 670 or 461 731

Warta Insurance and Reinsurance
Towarzystwo Ubezpieczen i
Reasekuracji
ul. Traugutta 5a
00 916 Warsaw
Tel: 010 4822 200 311
Tlx: 813 549

BANKS
Agrobank
ul. Grochowska 262
04 398 Warsaw
Tel: 010 4822 107 575
Tlx: 816 817

Bank Gdański
ul. Targ Drzewny 1
80 958 Gdańsk
Tel: 010 4858 311 611

Bank Handlowy
(Commercial Bank)
ul. Chalubinskiego 8

00 950 Warsaw
Tel: 010 4822 303 000
Tlx: 814 811

Deutsche Bank
Hotel Europejski, rm 20
ul. Krakowskie Przedmieście 13
00 710 Warsaw
Tel: 010 4822 263 056
Tlx: 816 515
Fax: 010 4822 263 050

National Bank of Poland
ul. Świętokrzyska 11/21
00 950 Warsaw
Tel: 010 4822 200 321
Tlx: 814681 nbp pl
Fax: 010 4822 269 955

Panstwowy Bank Kredytowy
ul. Nowogrodzka 35/42
00 950 Warsaw
Tel: 010 4822 299 348

HOTELS
Europejski
ul. Krakowskie Przedmieście 13
00 710 Warsaw
Tel: 010 4822 265 051
Tlx: 814 704

Forum Hotel
ul. Nowogrodzka 24/26
00 511 Warsaw
Tel: 010 4822 210 271
Tlx: 813 615

Grand Hotel
Krucza 28
00 120 Warsaw
Tel: 010 4822 294 091
Tlx: 813 422

Holiday Inn
Zlota 2
00 120 Warsaw
Tel: 010 4822 200 341
Tlx: 817 418

Hotel Victoria Intercontinental
ul. Królewska 11
00 065 Warsaw
Tel: 010 4822 278 011
Tlx: 812 516

Marriott Hotel
Aleje Jerozolimskie 67/71
00 697 Warsaw
Tel: 010 4822 306 306
Tlx: 816 515
Fax: 010 4822 30 311

Novotel
Pierwszego Sierpnia 1
02 134 Warsaw
Tel: 010 4822 464 051
Tlx: 812 525

Cracowia Orbis Hotel
al Puszkina 1
30 111 Kraków
Tel: 010 4812 228 666
Tlx: 322 341

Holiday Inn Orbis
ul. Koniewa 7
30 150 Kraków
Tel: 010 4812 375 044
Tlx: 325 356

Orbis Merkury Hotel
ul Roosevelta 20
60 821 Poznań
Tel: 010 4861 40801
Tlx: 413 434

Orbis Polonez Hotel
54/58 Stalingradzka Avenue
61 967 Poznań
Tel: 010 4861 699 141
Tlx: 413 491

CAR HIRE
Avis
Hotel Victoria Intercontinental
(see above)

Budget
Marriott Hotel (see above)

Hertz
Hotel Victoria Intercontinental
(see above)

Hertz
International Airport
Warsaw
Tel: 010 4822 469 896

Orbis
ul. Nowogrodska 24
Warsaw
Tel: 010 4822 210 271

PRESS
Business News from Poland
Aleje Jerozolimskie 7
00 950 Warsaw
POB 898
Tel: 010 4822 216 306
Tlx: 817 720
Fax: 010 4822 297 069

Foreign Trade Enterprise
(Bi-monthly newspaper)
Ars Polona
PO Box 1001
ul. Krakowskie Przedmieście 7/9
00 068 Warsaw

Polish Economy News
Polish Technical Review
Information for Businessmen
Trading with Poland
Chamber of Foreign Trade
ul. Trebacka 4, POB 361
00 950 Warsaw
Tel: 010 4822 260 221
Tlx: 814 361 pihz pl

Polish Foreign Trade
Foreign Trade Publishing Co.
Wydawnictwo Handlu
Zagranicznego
ul. Kierbedzia 4
00 957 Warsaw

Tel: 010 4822 416 061
Tlx: 816 061

The Warsaw Voice
Ul. Bagatela 12
00–585 Warszawa
Tel: 010 4822 211 328
Tlx: 814 775

PRESS

Business Eastern Europe
Business International Ltd
40 Duke Street
London W1A 1DW
Tel: 071 493 6711
Fax: 071 491 2107

Business International
BI Customer Service Department
40 Duke Street
London W1A 1DW
Tel: 071 493 6711

East European Digest
(issued by the) London Chamber
of Commerce
69 Cannon Street
London EC4N 5AB
Tel: 071 248 4444

East European Markets
Chiltern Magazine Services
9a Market Square
Chesham
Bucks HP5 1HG
Tel: 0494 771 734
Fax: 0494 778 994

or

FT Business Information Ltd
Tower House
Southampton Street
London WC2E 7HA
Tel: 071 240 9391
Fax: 071 240 7946

Eastern Europe Times
1401 Wilson Blvd.

Suite 952
Arlington
VA 22209
USA

or

Leibnitzstrasse 75
1000 Berlin 12

East-West Bulletin (fortnightly
bulletin, statistics service)
46 avenue Albert-Elisabeth
B-1200 Brussels
Belgium
Tel: 010 322 736 1193/94
Tlx: 26005 b
Fax: 010 322 736 2843

Gazeta International
8 Brunswick Gardens
London W5 1AP

Hints to Exporters
DTI Export Publications
Admail 124
London SE1 9XF

Opportunities Briefing
International Freedom
Foundation (UK)
Suite 500
Chesham House
150 Regent St.
London W1R 5FA
Tel: 071 729 5664
Fax: 071 729 2934

Summary of World Broadcasts
BBC Monitoring
Weekly Economic Report
Eastern Europe
Subscriptions office
BBC Monitoring
Caversham Park
Reading RG4 8TZ

and of course the *Financial Times*,
The Economist, the *Wall Street
Journal*, *The Independent*, and other
quality dailies.

NOTES AND FURTHER READING

INTRODUCTION

[1] Data from a survey of the top fifty US and top fifty-eight European companies, carried out for management consultants KPMG European Business Centre in March 1990. See also, 'Changing attitudes to European business arising from developments in Eastern Europe', survey also carried out by KPMG, April 1990.
[2] *Politique étrangère: Est: année des éléctions*, January 1990, Institut français des relations internationales, Paris 1990. Article by Pascal Lorot, 'Le CAEM à l'épreuve de la perestroika'.

CHAPTER 1

[1] BBC's *Summary of World Broadcasts* (*SWB*), quoting varied sources, such as the Prague Home Service.
[2] Lloyds Bank Economic Survey of Europe, June 1990.
[3] *SWB*, 7 June 1990.
[4] The Group for Independent Social Analysis, reviewed in the *International Herald Tribune*, 9 March 1990.

CHAPTER 2

[1] At a conference organised by the International Freedom Foundation, 22 May 1990.
[2] Department of Trade and Industry, February 1990.
[3] *SWB*, 1 February 1990, citing Hungarian Telegraph Agency (MTI).
[4] *SWB*, 19 April 1990, citing MTI.
[5] Ferenc Fekete, 'Progress and Problems in Hungarian Agriculture', in *Hungary: The Second Decade of Economic Reform*, ed. Roger A. Clarke in the series, *Perspectives on Eastern Europe* (Longman 1989) p73.
[6] *SWB*, 3 May 1990, citing MTI.
[7] Ferenc Havasi, quoted in Paul Lendvai, *Hungary: the Art of Survival* (Tauris, London 1988) p98.
[8] Details from Lendvai, *Hungary*.
[9] *SWB*, 8 February 1990.
[10] *SWB*, 17 May 1990, citing MTI.

CHAPTER 3

[1] Ernst & Young, *Investors guide to Poland* (1990) p25.
[2] *Policy & Politics in Contemporary Poland: Reform, Failure and Crisis*, ed Jean Woodall (London, Francis Pinter 1982) p109.
[3] *Poland: The Economy in the 1980s*, ed Roger A. Clarke, in the series *Perspectives on Eastern Europe* (Longman, 1989).
[4] *SWB*, 24 May 1990, citing Warsaw Home Service.
[5] Figures from Statistical Yearbook 1987.
[6] *SWB*, 10 May 1990, citing Polish Press Agency.

CHAPTER 4

[1] *SWB*, 1 March 1990, citing Czechoslovak Press Agency.
[2] *SWB*, 28 June 1990.
[3] Sara Parkin, *Green Parties: An International Guide* (Heretic, London 1989).
[4] Figures given in a speech by Baroness Cox at a conference organised by the International Freedom Foundation, 22 May 1990.
[5] For background, see *The East European Motor Industry*, Special Report No. 1167, (The Economist Intelligence Unit, January 1989).
[6] *SWB*, 5 July 1990, citing Hungarian Telegraph Agency.
[7] Baroness Cox's speech, see note 4.
[8] *SWB*, 2 August 1990.
[9] Details from a survey on retail in Eastern Europe prepared by Price Waterhouse for the European Commission, 1990.

CHAPTER 5

[1] The following three paragraphs are based on a seminar given by Dr Bohuslav Klein, legal director of the Czechoslovak Chamber of Commerce at S.J Berwin & Co. on 23 April 1990.
[2] *Business Eastern Europe*, 1 October 1990.
[3] Conference organised by the International Freedom Foundation, 22 May 1990.
[4] Alfred Biec, Secretary of the Government Economic Committee, cited in *SWB*, 27 September 1990.
[5] More detailed information on counter-trade is available from *Countertrade Update*, Business International, £695 annual subscription.

CHAPTER 6

[1] Willy de Clercq, 'Promoting East European Reform', in *European Freedom Review*, 2, Spring 1990.
[2] Claus-Dieter Ehlermann, 'Aid to Poland and Hungary', in *European Affairs*, 4, 1989.
[3] DTI handbook p8–1.

CHAPTER 7

[1] Dr Yochanan Altman, 'UK–Eastern Europe Joint Ventures: What are the Management Issues?', September 1990.
[2] Survey into UK Management Attitudes into working in the Eastern Bloc and the USSR. Merton Associates/Transearch International, February 1990.
[3] *Business Eastern Europe*, 17 September 1990.
[4] Information on banks from *Countertrade Update*, Business International, December 1989.
[5] *SWB*, 27 September 1990, citing Czechoslovak Press Agency.

BIBLIOGRAPHY

ASH, T. Garton
We the People: The Revolution of '89 Witnessed in Warsaw, Budapest, Berlin and Prague
Granta/Penguin, 1990.
Business and Investment in Eastern Europe and the USSR (Documentation from seminar, 5 April 1990) Jones, Day, Ravis & Pogue, and Morgan Grenfell.
CLARKE, R.A. ed.
Hungary: The Second Decade of Economic Reform Longman, pbk., 1989.
CLARKE R.A. ed.
Poland: The Economy in the 1980s Longman, pbk., 1989.
Czechoslovakia (Country profile) Economist Intelligence Unit, 1990. Annual.
Czechoslovakia (Country report) Economist Intelligence Unit, 1990. Quarterly.
Czechoslovakia: Paving the Way to a Free Economy 1990. KPMG Peat Marwick McLintock, 1 Puddle Dock, London EC4V 3PD. 071 236 8000.
Czechoslovakia Business International. Monthly.
Doing Business with Eastern Europe: Czechoslovakia Business International. Monthly.
Doing Business with Eastern Europe: Hungary Business International. Monthly.
Doing Business with Eastern Europe: Poland Business International. Monthly.
Eastern Europe and the USSR; Economic Structure and Analysis (Regional reference series) Economist Intelligence Unit, 1990.
Eastern Europe and the USSR: A Guide to Foreign Investment Legislation 1990. KPMG Peat Marwick McLintock, as above.
Economic Survey of Europe 1990. Annual, free. Available from Economic Dept., Lloyds Bank, 71 Lombard St., London EC3V 9EE. 071 626 1500.
HERRMAN, A.H.
Economic and Legal Problems of Transition to Market Economy 1990. Available from Centre for Commercial Law Studies, Queen Mary & Westfield College, University of London, Mile End Rd., London E1 4NS. 081 975 5555.
Investment in Hungary 1990. KPMG Peat Marwick McLintock, as above.
Investors' Guide to Poland 1990. Available from Ernst & Young, Becket House, Lambeth Palace Rd., London SE1 4XY. 071 928 2000.
LENDVAI, P.
Hungary: The Art of Survival Tauris, 1988.
LUKOWICZ, M. ed.
Legal Framework of Joint Venture Available from Foreign Investment Agency, Plac Powstańców, 00950, Warsaw, Poland.
OBSERVER
Tearing Down the Curtain: The People's Revolution in Eastern Europe ed. N. Hawkes. Hodder, 1990.
Poland (Country report) Economist Intelligence Unit. Quarterly.
Politique étrangère. No. 90–1. Est: année des élections (Institut français des relations internationales) Paris: A Collin, 1990.
SCHREIBER, T. and BARRY, F. eds.
L'URSS et l'Europe de l'est en 1989. (Notes et études documentaires no. 4891/2) Paris: Documentation française, 1989.
SWORD, K. ed.
Times Guide to Eastern Europe Times Bks., pbk., 1990.

INDEX